DIGITAL RETRO

DIGITAL RETRO

GORDON LAING

ILEX

DEDICATED TO
Mum and Dad, for sparking my passion with a Sinclair
ZX81, and continuing to encourage me with
subsequent models, despite their increasingly obvious
realization that none was for educational purposes.
Nicki, for encouraging me to write this book.

contents

004_05

First published in the United Kingdom in 2004 by

I L E X

The Old Candlemakers
West Street
Lewes
East Sussex BN7 2NZ

ILEX is an imprint of The Ilex Press Ltd
Visit us on the web at:
www.ilex-press.com

Copyright © 2004 The Ilex Press Limited

This book was conceived by
ILEX, Cambridge, England

ILEX Editorial, Lewes:
Publisher: Alastair Campbell
Executive Publisher: Sophie Collins
Creative Director: Peter Bridgewater
Editorial Director: Steve Luck
Editor: Adam Juniper
Design Manager: Tony Seddon
Designer: Jonathan Raimes
Artwork Administrator: Joanna Clinch

ILEX Research, Cambridge:
Development Art Director: Graham Davis
Technical Art Editor: Nicholas Rowland

British Library Cataloguing-in-Publication Data
A catalogue record for this book is available
from the British Library

ISBN 1-904705-39-1

Printed and bound in China

For more information on this title please visit:
www.retruk.web-linked.com

digital : retro

introduction

The period between the mid-Seventies and the late Eighties was completely unique in the history of computing. Long before Microsoft and Intel dominated the scene, a multitude of home computers were battling for supremacy in a melting point that would shape the IT industry for years to come.

Especially during the early Eighties, it seemed a new computer was released almost every month. Machines from established technology giants were taken as seriously as models developed by a handful of enthusiasts.

The one thing they all had in common, though, would later lead to their demise: incompatibility. Virtually every new machine was incompatible with the last and had little or no intention of communicating with anything but its own kind – very much like their owners, who passionately defended their computers with a belief that often verged on the religious.

It was a strategy that couldn't last, yet over a period of around fifteen years, it was responsible for an unprecedented degree of variety and innovation. *Digital Retro* is the story behind the computers of this era, their creators and the inspiration that drove them to take on their rivals.

What inspired Sinclair to build the ZX80? How did Acorn land the BBC Micro contract? Was the Commodore 64 genuinely better than the Spectrum? Could a machine best known as the Welsh Computer really succeed? Why did Microsoft and the world's biggest Japanese companies fail with their first home computer, and, while we're at it, what's the real story behind Apple and Atari? Among these big names you'll also read about less familiar companies like Oric, Tangerine and Dragon.

Digital Retro reveals the stories behind the most popular home computers of the Eighties, which, while often modest in capability, introduced many people to the joys of computing. While this book concentrates on the low-cost machines designed for home use, it also includes key game consoles and business computers that influenced future standards.

The computers' designers have been interviewed where possible, avoiding popular myths, and we photographed original models for reference. Accompanying each machine are its vital statistics, including details of its launch or original announcement. In each case, we've stated the launch date and price in the computer's country of origin and local currency.

While we've made every effort to ensure the historical accuracy of this book, memories inevitably fade while old rivalries often remain. It's also true what they say about history being written by the winners. Still, a hearteningly large number of the original designers were happy to share their memories, and as such, *Digital Retro* hopes to present an honest, detailed and accurate account of each machine. If we've missed anything or left anyone out, please forgive us.

Personally speaking, *Digital Retro* has given me a chance to relive a period I remember with great fondness. Like many my age, my first experience of home computing was with Sinclair's ZX80, back in 1980.

Toward the end of my formative years at Cherry Tree Primary School in the small town of Romiley, in northwest England, my class learned of a competition to win a computer. Our interest sparked by a cardboard model of a ZX80, we entered and won. I'm afraid to say my contribution was far from the greatest, a fact reflected by my position on the very edge of a class photo, subsequently cropped out when published in the *Manchester Evening News*.

The machine itself, though, while physically diminutive, utterly captivated me for months to come. The following year, I nagged my parents into buying its successor, the ZX81, and later, the ubiquitous ZX Spectrum. Over the years, I graduated to a Commodore 64 and an Atari ST before buying my first really serious computer, a Macintosh. Today I'm a dual-platform kind of guy, using both Macs and PCs.

As someone who writes about modern technology, the interesting thing for me is remembering the passion with which owners defended their computers in the Eighties. Fights would break out in school playgrounds over whether the ZX Spectrum was better than the Commodore 64. Today, while some Mac-versus-PC arguments can become pretty heated, it's hard to imagine coming to blows over them.

Yes, today's personal computers may allow us to do more than we could ever have imagined, but the fervour for the actual hardware has waned considerably. So with a nostalgic tear in your eye, join me on a journey back to a more innocent age, where rubber keyboards, strained beeps and a palette of 16 colours was considered state of the art. Welcome to *Digital Retro* and the birth of personal computing.

a brief history of computers

008_9

Personal computers may dominate today's IT landscape, but in evolutionary terms, they're positively youthful. Large departmental computing systems have been around since the mid-1940s, while the concept of automatic calculating machines can be traced back to the 1820s.

Charles Babbage is widely regarded as the father of computing, thanks to his invention, the Analytical Engine. Babbage was born on Boxing Day 1791, in Teignmouth, Devonshire, in southwest England. In 1822, five years after receiving his MA from Cambridge University, Babbage wrote to the president of the Royal Society with a plan for a machine that could calculate and print mathematical tables. The following year, the Chancellor of the Exchequer granted Babbage the funds to proceed with his Difference Engine.

Over the following decade, Babbage attempted to build the Difference Engine, but fabrication and funding proved troublesome. Toward the end of this period, Babbage proposed a more powerful version, accurate to twenty decimal places compared to the original's six. In 1833, though, Babbage devised an entirely new machine he claimed was capable of performing any mathematical operation; he called it the Analytical Engine.

While neither the Analytical nor Difference Engines were built during Babbage's lifetime, their concepts and proposed means of execution paved the way for modern computing. Babbage died in 1871.

As the century drew to a close, the first practically realized computers were used to process huge quantities of information for governmental applications. In 1890, statistician and German immigrant to the United States Herman Hollerith won a contest held by the US Census Bureau to find a more efficient way of handling its data. Hollerith's punched-card solution inspired him to later form his own Tabulating Machine Company

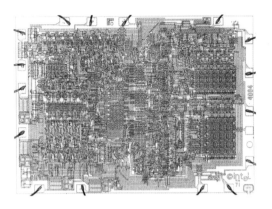

The Intel 4004B microprocessor handled 4000 instructions a second. Gordon Moore, Intel executive and originator of the rule that bears his name, described it as "one of the most revolutionary products in the history of mankind". For the record, Moore's law actually states "the number of transistors the industry will be able to place on a computer chip will double every couple of years".

in 1896, which, following several mergers, evolved into IBM in 1924. Twelve years later, in 1936, British mathematician Alan Turing conceived a hypothetical device that could infallibly recognize undecidable propositions. His Turing Machine could perform functions in a sequence of discrete steps and record them onto tape for later analysis.

By incorporating input and output, the storage of programs and processing control, Turing's theoretical machine became the basis for all digital computers. Turing later joined the team at England's Bletchley Park that cracked the Germans' Enigma code during World War II.

In the decade following the end of that war, several mammoth calculating and computing machines were created.

In 1944, IBM – in conjunction with six years of work with Harvard University – finished the Automatic Sequence Controlled Calculator, also known as the Mark I. Over fifty feet long and weighing five tons, it could perform an automatic division in around twelve seconds.

Two years later, work finished on the ENIAC I (Electrical Numerical Integrator And Calculator), commissioned by the US military to calculate artillery firing tables. Taking three years to build, and costing taxpayers $500,000, John Mauchly and John Presper Eckert's machine contained 17,468 tubes, 70,000 resistors, 10,000 capacitors, 1,500 relays and 6,000 manual switches.

With a footprint of 1,800 square feet, weight of 30 tons and power consumption of 160 kilowatts, the ENIAC I caused brownouts in Philadelphia when powered up. In one second, though, it could perform 5,000 additions, 357 multiplications or 38 divisions.

In the year of the ENIAC I's launch, Sir Frederick Williams and Tom Kilburn were working on storing information on vacuum tubes, while the former chaired the

department of electrical engineering at Manchester University in England. Williams managed to store one bit of information on a Cathode-ray tube, which Kilburn later improved to an impressive 2,048 bits.

In 1948, Kilburn designed and built a computer around the new tube technology, nicknamed the Baby. It had a computing speed of 1.2 milliseconds per instruction. Over the following years, computers accelerated in performance but continued to rely on power-hungry vacuum tubes that needed replacing on a regular basis.

During the early Fifties, John Bardeen, Walter Brattain and William Shockley of Bell Telephone Labs were conducting research on crystals to find a replacement for tubes. The team finally tried a purer substance for the contact points, and came up with the first transistor amplifier. They were awarded the Nobel Prize in Physics in 1956.

In 1957, Sherman Mills Fairchild, founder of Fairchild Camera and Instrument Corporation, sponsored a small group of young Californian scientists to develop a new process for manufacturing transistors. Two of the scientists working on the problem were Gordon Moore and Robert Noyce, the latter one of the founders of the new Fairchild Semiconductor company.

Their ultimate goal was to find a way to integrate the previously separate transistors, resistors, capacitors and wires that made up a complete circuit onto a single crystal or chip made from semiconducting material. Noyce spent two years developing a solution, but was unaware that Jack Kilby of Texas Instruments was working on the same problem.

They both applied for patents in 1959, with Kilby choosing the name Germanium for his semiconductor, and Noyce opting for Silicon. After several years of legal wrangling, the two companies agreed to cross-license their respective technologies.

a brief history of computers

010_11

In 1961, Fairchild produced the first commercial integrated circuit, with Texas Instruments using its first chips for US Air Force computers. Texas Instruments later used its integrated circuits in the first pocket calculators, whose invention is credited to Jack Kilby.

During the Sixties, computers became increasingly widespread, but they typically remained room-sized mainframes or minicomputers resembling large kitchen appliances. Toward the end of the decade, though, a new company was formed that would pioneer the technologies allowing computers to be placed on the desktop.

In the spring of 1968, Gordon Moore and Robert Noyce decided to leave Fairchild and start their own company, intending to design and manufacture large-scale integrated (LSI) memory. Noyce typed up his own business plan and approached venture capitalist Art Rock, who originally helped fund Fairchild Semiconductor. Rock came up with $2.5 million, and NM Electronics was formed that July.

NM wasn't the best choice of names, so Noyce and Moore later opted for Integrated Electronics, and shortened it to Intel. Coincidentally, a hotel chain already owned the name, but it was happy to sell.

Around the same time, the US military set up the ARPAnet to link their nationwide array of mainframe and minicomputers. The ARPAnet was also employed by academic and research communities, and while it remained a private resource for several decades, it later became the backbone of the internet.

Intel started life as planned by producing memory: its first product was the "3101 Schottky bipolar 64-bit static random access memory (SRAM) chip". While successful, its longer-term fortunes would be changed by another technology.

Japanese company Busicom approached Intel to design twelve custom chips for a new calculator, a project Intel agreed to take on without the resources to complete

The Apple 1 was not supplied with a case, so hobbyists had to construct their own. Many constructed theirs from wood.

it. Fortunately, Intel engineer Ted Hoff reckoned a single chip could actually do the job of them all. Noyce, Moore and Busicom liked Hoff's thinking, and backed development.

Hoff's plan was to design a general-purpose logic chip that could be programmed by software, rather than by burning instructions directly into hardware. Intel's Federico Faggin and Stan Mazor, along with Busicom's Masatoshi Shima, worked on Hoff's plan; in 1971, after nine months of work, the first microprocessor was born.

Intel's 4004 microprocessor measured an eighth of an inch wide by a sixth of an inch long, consisted of 2,300 transistors and ran at 0.1 MHz. This may sound extremely modest compared to the 42 million transistors on the Pentium 4 processor, but back in 1971, the 4004 boasted the same computing power as the earlier ENIAC I, which filled 3,000 cubic feet with almost 18,000 vacuum tubes.

The 4004 was undoubtedly a revolution, but one owned by Busicom. Intel negotiated with the Japanese and bought the 4004's design and marketing rights for $60,000; Busicom went bankrupt a short time later. It wasn't, however, a foregone conclusion that anyone would want a microprocessor: Despite now owning the 4004, Intel had to persuade people to use it.

The turning point both for Intel and the entire IT industry came in 1974, when Intel's latest 2MHz 8080 microprocessor was selected as the brains of the MITS Altair computer kit. While kits had existed before, the Altair was the first to employ components that could be sourced relatively easily by enthusiasts. Consequently, the Altair is widely regarded as being the first personal computer, and it had an Intel inside.

The MITS Altair became the cover star of the January 1975 issue of *Practical Electronics* magazine and had a profound impact on many who saw it. Bill Gates (later to drop out of Harvard) and friend Paul Allen (then at Honeywell) adapted the BASIC programming language to run on the Altair, licensed it to MITS in early 1975 and officially shipped it in July that year as BASIC 2.0. Allen was later taken on by MITS as director of software development, and Gates followed afterwards, and spoke of their partnership as one with Micro-soft – at the time, complete with hyphen.

The Altair also starred at the first meeting of the Homebrew Computer Club on 5th March, 1975, held for West Coast US enthusiasts in a local private garage. While impressed by the Altair, the Homebrew members found flaws, and many began to develop alternatives, still using the powerful but expensive Intel 8080 microprocessor.

Homebrew member Stephen Wozniak, who worked at Hewlett Packard's handheld-calculator division at the time, was also inspired to build his own computer, but with a much cheaper chip. Chuck Peddle of MOS Technologies had recently developed a low-priced microprocessor called the 6502, which he first sold from a hotel suite during the Westcon show in San Francisco, in September 1975. Wozniak acquired one and almost single-handedly assembled a new computer in his friend Steve Jobs's garage. The pair registered the company name Apple on 1st April, 1976, and launched Wozniak's basic machine as the Apple I.

While Intel later scored the ultimate goal by having its 8088 microprocessor used in the first IBM PC, it's important not to underestimate the importance of Chuck Peddle's 6502. This chip not only powered the Apple I and its successor the Apple II; it was also employed by countless machines throughout the late Seventies and early Eighties, including models created by Atari, Acorn, Commodore and even Nintendo.

Intel's 8080 and 8088 were important chips at the higher end, but Peddle's 6502 was arguably the catalyst that kicked off the affordable home-computer revolution. Over the next fifteen years, an enormous variety of machines was launched, each hoping for fame and fortune – until one standard eventually gained sufficient momentum to utterly dominate the planet. What follows are their stories.

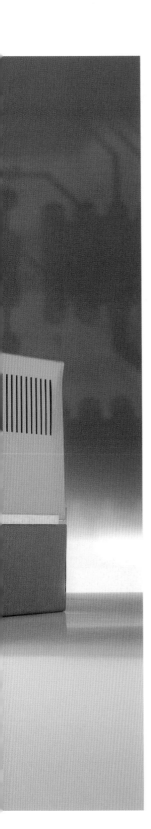

Practical Electronics magazine was halfway through preparing a computer kit article when a rival magazine beat them to it with a project called the Mark 8. *Practical Electronics'* editorial director Art Salsberg and technical director Les Solomon realized they had to up the ante in order to successfully counter the Mark 8 article.

Ed Roberts was an existing contributor to *Practical Electronics* and keen to build a kit computer. Salsberg and Solomon contacted Roberts and discovered his machine would be more sophisticated and better-looking than the haywire rigs proposed by others; crucially, Roberts reckoned he would have it ready in time for the January 1975 issue.

Roberts based his machine around Intel's new 8080 processor, running at 2 MHz. Intel normally charged $300 for the 8080 when purchased in small numbers, but Roberts secured a deal to buy larger numbers with cosmetic defects at just $75 each. This price would allow Roberts to deliver a kit for less than $400, but he'd only break even if he sold over 200 units.

The name was actually coined by Solomon's twelve-year-old daughter, who was watching *Star Trek* at the time. The episode in question was "Amok Time", in which Spock and Kirk are forced to fight to the death over a bride for the Vulcan. The *Enterprise* was originally on its way to planet Altair 6.

MITS
Altair 8800

Manufacturer: MITS
Model: Altair 8800

Launched: January 1975
Country of Origin: USA

COMPANY HISTORY

Micro Instrumentation Telemetry Systems, or MITS for short, was founded in the late Sixties by Ed Roberts, and was based in Albuquerque, New Mexico. Roberts had become an expert in electronics while serving in the air force and later went into business building calculators and radio-controlled models. During the early Seventies, a number of technical magazines published guides on building electronics projects, but when the first microprocessors were launched, each wanted to be first with a kit-computer article. The first computer construction project to be published was actually not the MITS Altair, but the Mark 8 by Jonathan Titus in the July 1974 edition of *Radio Electronics Magazine*. The Mark 8 employed an Intel 8008 processor but is not widely credited as being the first personal computer because it was presented to potential customers as a shopping list with instructions on assembly. Self-assembly was common at this time, but proved impossible for many. In contrast, MITS would supply the parts required to build an Altair.

SPECIFICATION

CPU model: Intel 8080
Speed: 2 MHz
RAM: 256 Byte memory cards
Special features: 16 expansion slots
Local price at launch: $397 kit-form, $498 pre-assembled

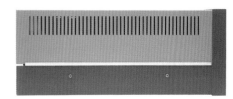

1975

MITS
Altair 8800

014_15

Manufacturer: MITS
Model: Altair 8800

WHAT HAPPENED NEXT

Sporting a sharp-looking box with toggle switches and **LEDs**, the Altair 8800 was featured on the cover of January 1975's *Practical Electronics* magazine. A strike on the railways, however, meant the original Altair got lost, forcing the magazine to photograph a dummy unit instead. This gave Roberts a chance to improve his system, so the model that went on sale to readers featured a superior expansion bus. Over the issues in which the kit was featured, readers ordered an estimated 2,000 Altair 8800s, allowing Roberts to more than break even. In 1977, Roberts sold **MITS** to Pertec Computer Corp. for $6 million, then went on to pursue his true love medicine.

The 8800 and 8800b models without the Turnkey had an array of science fiction-like flickering switches on the front panel, and users could debug their programs by switching to "slow" mode – about five cycles per second – and watching the program operate step-by-step.

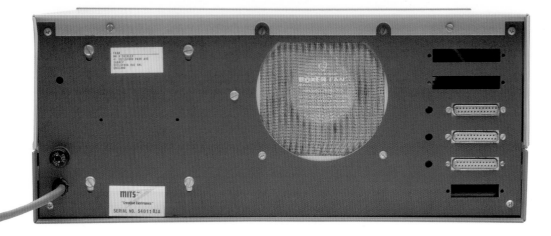

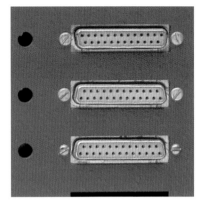

INPUT/OUTPUT
1. 15x S-100 card slots
2. Serial Port

All components, including
memory and CPU, had to be
attached to the bus. The 8800b
included the Turnkey module
(8080A CPU, serial port, 1K
RAM and 1K ROM). Unlike the
original 8800, the Turnkey
version set addresses using
DIP switches.

DID YOU KNOW?
The MITS Altair 8800 was an incredibly
influential system, not least because it
was arguably the first personal
computer. Bill Gates and Paul Allen
adapted their version of **BASIC** to run
on the Altair and licensed it to **MITS** in
early 1975: It shipped in July that year
as BASIC 2.0 and was Microsoft's first
commercial product. The Altair was
also popular at the Homebrew
Computer Club in Santa Clara,
California, where member Stephen
Wozniak saw it. Watching unreliable
demonstrations of the Altair and how
easily other members could fix or
improve on it inspired Wozniak and his
friend Steve Jobs to build the Apple I.

Commodore PET 2001

During the early Seventies, Commodore was successful at building calculators, but it was hit hard when component suppliers like Texas Instruments began assembling them internally. By 1975, Commodore had fallen from $60 million in sales to $5 million in losses, and company owner Jack Tramiel vowed to never again be at the mercy of component suppliers. Close to insolvency in 1976, Tramiel borrowed $3 million from Canada's Irving Gold and bought MOS Technologies, thereby acquiring two valuable assets: engineer Chuck Peddle and his 6502 processor.

Peddle had worked earlier on the expensive 6800 processor at Motorola, but he designed the 6502 – which cost almost ten times less – to meet manufacturers' requests for a chip costing just $20. Once acquired by Commodore, Peddle sold a computer idea to the company's engineering manager Andre Sousan, a project Tramiel initially backed into limited production. A deadline of six months to produce the first machine was set.

Peddle's team, which included Tramiel's son Leonard as software tester, created an all-in-one system with built-in keyboard, cassette drive and nine-inch monitor, along with 4KB of RAM and, of course, a 6502 processor. They called it the PET 2001, officially short for Personal Electronic Transactor, but also cashing in on the Pet Rock fad, while respectfully nodding to Arthur C. Clarke.

Manufacturer: Commodore	**Launched:** January 1977
Model: PET 2001	**Country of Origin:** USA

SPECIFICATION

CPU model: MOS 6502
Speed: 1MHz
RAM: 4KB
Special features: Built-in 9in monitor and tape drive
Local price at launch: $495

COMPANY HISTORY

Commodore was founded by Jack Tramiel, born Idek Tramielski in Lodz, Poland, in 1929. Tramiel survived six years in Auschwitz and other concentration camps during World War II. Two years after liberation, he emigrated to America, becoming a repairman at a New York City lamp shop. In 1948, he joined the US Army, where he was trained to repair office equipment while stationed at Fort Dix. After serving four years, Tramiel took a job at a New York repair shop and used his contacts to continue servicing army typewriters, but when the owner refused to give him a raise, Tramiel decided to start his own company. In 1953, the same year he became a US citizen, Tramiel and his friend Manny Kapp opened their own repair shop in the Bronx. Wanting a name with a military ring, but knowing General and Admiral were already in use, they called it Commodore Portable Typewriter. When US import regulations later prevented Tramiel from importing Olivetti typewriter parts, he relocated to Toronto, Canada, where in 1955 he founded Commodore Business Machines, or CBM.

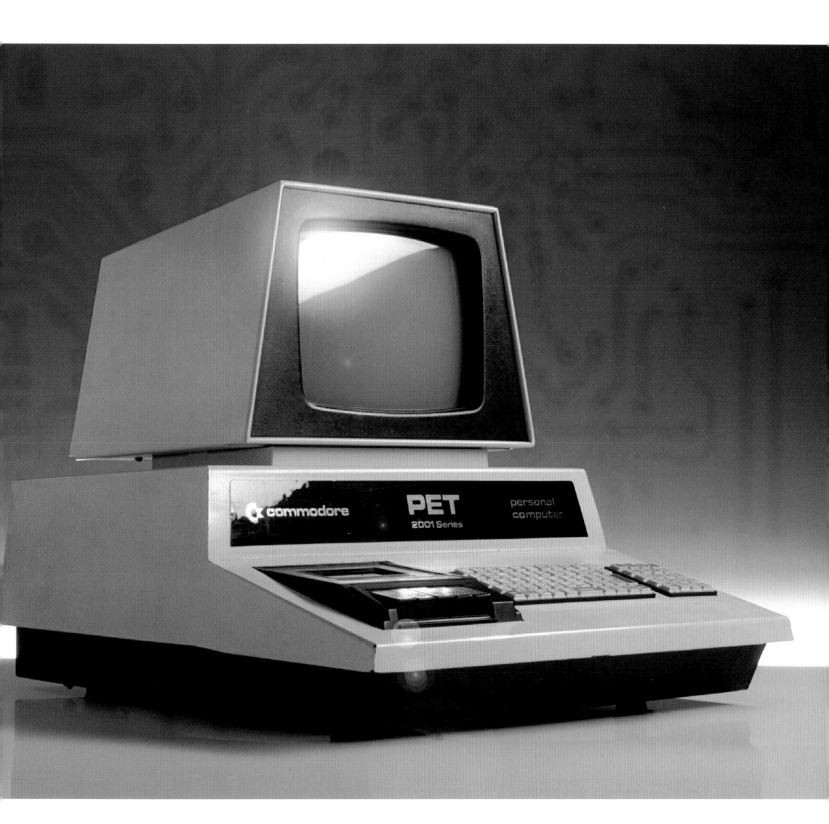

1977

Commodore
PET 2001

Manufacturer: Commodore
Model: PET 2001

Early in its life, the PET earned one of the ultimate accolades for a gadget of the time: an appearance in *Playboy* magazine. The article portrayed the PET as a device for the gentleman sophisticate, though it was pictured with a PET graphic of the Playboy Bunny on the screen.

WHAT HAPPENED NEXT

Inundated by orders, Tramiel quickly raised the 4KB PET price to $595, in turn encouraging sales of the $795 8KB model. Advance sales funded initial production, with Jack promising delivery "in 120 days or your money back" – although no one ever requested the refund. In subsequent years, Commodore released several upgraded models, the first swapping the original "chicklet" keyboard for a proper full-size model; this in turn left no room for the internal cassette drive. The final model was the SuperPET. In the meantime, Peddle's legendary 6502 had been employed by countless computers and games consoles, while Peddle himself left to form Sirius in 1980.

INPUT/OUTPUT

1. IEEE 488
2. Parallel Port
3. 8-bit user port
4. Cassette port within case

The all-in-one design gave Commodore a much more consumer-friendly product than those before it, but it did have some idiosyncrasies – not least that the RAM chips could get hot enough to creep out of their slots over time.

DID YOU KNOW?
Chuck Peddle may have met his deadline for delivering the PET, but the prototype shown at a January 1977 trade show, not to mention featured on several magazine covers, had a chassis made from wood.

Apple launched its first computer in 1976 but needed sales to develop a follow-up. The company's first big customer was Paul Terrell, who, after seeing the Apple I at a Homebrew club meeting, was persuaded by Apple co-founder Steve Jobs to sell fifty completed boards at his Byte computer shop. Unable to afford the parts required, Jobs convinced an electronics firm to give him thirty days' credit.

Apple now had money in the bank, but not enough for the expansion Jobs had in mind. While searching for venture capital, he met Mike Markkula, a former Intel employee who'd retired at the age of thirty-three. Impressed by the two Steves and their first product, Markkula persuaded others this was a company worth investing in, hired Mike Scott as its CEO, and became one third of Apple. Crucially, he also convinced its technical genius Wozniak to give up the day job at HP.

Wozniak began work developing the Apple I's successor. Colour was high on his wish list, despite it being highly unusual back then. In the meantime, Jobs studied consumer-appliance design and decided to break away from the traditional metal case. He hired Jerry Mannock to design a beige plastic case with rounded corners and commissioned Rob Janov to design the now-familiar striped Apple logo. The final months may have been frantic, but the Apple II met its deadline and was shown at the first West Coast Computer Faire, in San Francisco in May 1977.

Apple II

Manufacturer: Apple
Model: II

Launched: January 1977
Country of Origin: USA

COMPANY HISTORY

Apple was founded on April Fools' day 1976 by Steve Jobs and Stephen Wozniak, who had met through mutual friend Bill Fernandez three years earlier. Fernandez had invited Jobs over to take a look at a computer he and Wozniak had built in his parent's garage; they called it the Cream Soda Computer after their favourite drink. At the time, Jobs and Wozniak were 16 and 20 years old.

After dropping out of the University of California at Berkeley, Wozniak joined Fernandez at HP's handheld calculator division. Jobs joined Atari, where he persuaded boss Nolan Bushnell to let him program a game the latter had devised. Bushnell agreed, but Jobs got Wozniak to help him program it after hours. The game became Breakout, one of Atari's big hits. Wozniak had also been attending the Homebrew Computer Club, where he and other hobbyists were inspired to build their own machines after seeing the MITS Altair 8800. Equipped with a new 6502 processor bought personally from Chuck Peddle at the 1975 Westcon show, Wozniak almost single-handedly built a computer in Jobs' garage. It was only a circuit board, but the Apple I was born.

SPECIFICATION

CPU model: 6502
Speed: 1 MHz
RAM: 4KB
Special features: Expansion slots, colour capability, rounded plastic case
Local price at launch: $1195

The plastic case was a major factor in the Apple II's commercial success, as it helped create the image of a consumer-friendly device, which Apple made central to the advertising. It was the first computer company to advertise outside the computer/hobbyist press. National campaigns featured the Apple II on kitchen tables, on Thomas Jefferson's desk and even serving as Adam's fig leaf in the Garden of Eden.

Apple II

022_23

Model: Apple II
Launched: January 1977

WHAT HAPPENED NEXT

Apple secured a small but prominent stand at the West Coast Computer Faire, and over 300 orders were placed for its new machine within a few days. Sales steadily grew for the Apple II, which most considered superior to its competitors, the Commodore PET and TRS-80; but it took a piece of software to really make a difference. Dan Bricklin came up with the idea of an electronic spreadsheet in 1978, and he and Bob Frankston later wrote it for the Apple II. Launched as VisiCalc in 1979, it was the first killer application for personal computers and was, at first, available only for the Apple II. Mike Scott estimated it was responsible for over 25,000 Apple II sales by the end of 1980.

Apple also began carving out its niche in the US education market with the Apple II. Apple's own marketing featured the Logo programming language, in which graphics could be created using simple commands. The machine was also sold in cases painted black by Bell & Howell.

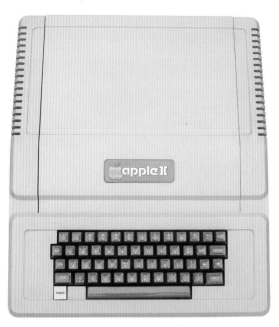

The motherboard featured eight expansion slots, so that the user could expand the system by simply lifting the lid and adding a card. Apple were keen to promote the simplicity of adding "Apple's smart peripherals", hinting at plug-and-play in their sales material.

INPUT/OUTPUT

1 Video out (composite)
2 8 expansion slots
3 Tape recorder
4 Paddles

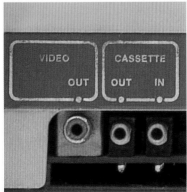

DID YOU KNOW?

While working at HP, Stephen Wozniak started a business called Dial-a-joke. Every morning he'd record a joke into his home answering machine which people subsequently called. At its peak, over 2000 people called per day, making it one of the most dialled numbers in the Bay Area; sadly Wozniak made no money from it, since at the time noone knew how to bill for such calls.

Wozniak's Dial-a-joke phone number was 255-6666. Repeating numbers appealed to Wozniak, and when Jobs suggested a retail price of $650 for the Apple I, Woz countered with $666, then $666.66.

Atari VCS

With the success of the Pong arcade machine, Atari engineers Bob Brown and Harold Lee developed a home version that became a best-seller when launched in 1975. Other dedicated consoles followed, but each required custom circuits with high development costs. With Atari's management wanting increasingly complex games, a more flexible approach became necessary.

Steve Mayer and Larry Emmons had previously formed Cyan, which provided consultancy to Atari before being acquired as its research and development arm. During the summer of 1975, Mayer and Ron Milner began sketching ideas for a programmable console, but they needed a low-cost processor to power it.

As luck would have it, Chuck Peddle introduced his affordable new 6502 processor at the annual Westcon show that September. Mayer and Milner met with Peddle and discovered that the 6502 almost perfectly matched their requirements. After Mayer and Milner created the first design, Joe Decuir was hired to debug it in time for a demonstration for Atari founder Nolan Bushnell and *Pong*-programmer Al Alcorn the following February. Decuir subsequently moved to Los Gatos, California, where he worked with Jay Miner to complete the system using a 6502 derivative called the 6507. The project was then code-named Stella, after the brand of French bicycle Decuir owned.

Manufacturer: Atari	**Launched:** June 1977
Name: Video Computer System	**Country of Origin:** USA

SPECIFICATION

CPU model: 6507
Speed: 1.2MHz
RAM: 128 Bytes
Special features: Supplied with two joysticks and two analog paddles. Wood panel effect
Local price at launch: $199

COMPANY HISTORY

Nolan Bushnell and Ted Dabney founded Atari on 27th June, 1972. The name Atari comes from its founders playing the Japanese game of Go, in which the word is called out like "check" would be in chess. Bushnell is widely regarded as the father of video games, but two products played a great influence. First was Spacewar, which Bushnell played on DEC mainframes while studying for his electrical engineering degree at the University of Utah. After graduating in 1968 and taking jobs at Ampex, Bushnell and Dabney created their own version of Spacewar for self-contained arcade cabinets, which they called Computer Space. After leaving Ampex to form Atari, they hired engineer Al Alcorn to build Pong from Bushnell's idea for video tennis. Bushnell's second and more contentious influence was the Magnavox Odyssey console. Launched in March 1972, the Odyssey featured a Ping-Pong game developed by Ralph Baer, Bill Rusch and Bill Harrison. According to Baer, Bushnell attended a Magnavox demonstration in May 1972, previous to launching the similar Atari *Pong*. Whatever *Pong*'s influence, it was an enormous hit, and Atari subsequently produced many seminal arcade coin-ops including Breakout, Battlezone, Asteroids and Centipede.

digital : retro

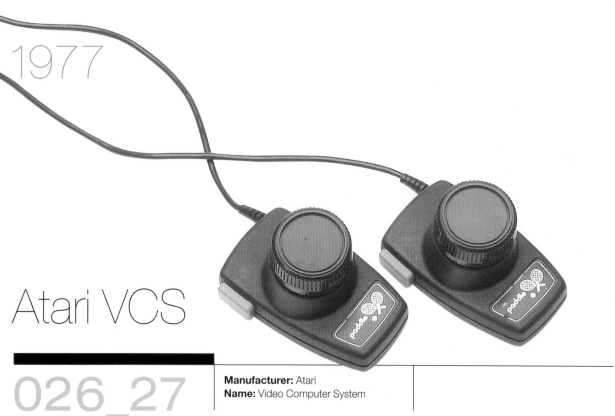

026_27

Atari VCS

Manufacturer: Atari
Name: Video Computer System

The switches at either side of the cartridge slot, "left difficulty" and "right difficulty", hark back to the days of *Pong* where players could be individually handicapped. The "colour/b&w" switch could also be used by games for other purposes, such as a pause mode, and the "game select" switch allowed the user to cycle through game variations (there were 112 on the *Space Invaders* cartridge).

WHAT HAPPENED NEXT

Atari announced its new Video Computer System, VCS, at the June 1977 Consumer Electronics Show. It was sold with a pair of joysticks, two analog paddles and the game Combat – originally a prototype by Decuir that Wagner later turned into a commercial title.

Despite its many games, each with countless variations, the VCS had a slow start. Its big break came in 1980 when Atari negotiated the exclusive home rights for Taito's *Space Invaders*. Big-name licensing continued as the VCS acquired competitors in the console market. Bushnell sold Atari to Warner in 1976 and resigned in 1978. Miner (and later Decuir) left in 1979 to start work what would become the Amiga. Crane and colleagues also left in 1979 to form Activision.

Featuring a large black plastic grill fronted with mock wood, the VCS's design owed something to the stereo systems of the era, a look that made entertainment equipment feel like it was part of the furniture.

DID YOU KNOW?

During the early Eighties, the licensing of major arcade games and movies became big business. Unfortunately, many of the home conversions were either rushed or lacking in playability. The highly anticipated *Pac Man* was a case in point, but most infamous of all was Atari's licensing of the movie *ET*.

Legend has it that Atari paid millions of dollars for the rights to produce an *ET* game, but after highly disappointing sales, the company allegedly dumped hundreds of thousands or even millions of unsold cartridges in a New Mexico landfill. While this story is officially denied, disappointing sales from expensive licenses like *Pac Man* and *ET* were a major factor in the video games crash of the mid-Eighties.

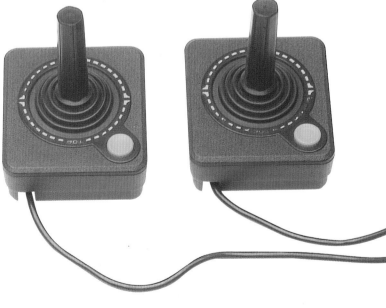

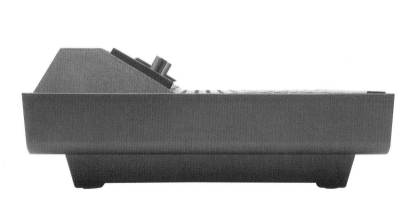

Tandy RadioShack TRS-80

During the early Seventies, the CB-radio craze allowed RadioShack to enjoy sufficient growth that by 1975, its parent, the Tandy Corporation, dealt exclusively with electronics. When the CB market collapsed, Tandy searched for the next trend.

Don French, a West Coast buyer for Tandy and computer hobbyist, was convinced personal computers would be the next big thing, but his boss suspected they'd just be another risky fad. French later visited National Semiconductor with John Roach, Tandy's vice president of manufacturing, where they were briefed by Steve Leininger.

French and Roach wanted to hire Leininger as a consultant, but National wouldn't reveal his personal contact details. Later the pair stopped at Paul Terrell's Byte store, where they were understandably surprised to find Leininger working as a night clerk. Four weeks later, Leininger was invited to Tandy at Fort Worth and subsequently offered a job.

After he played around with various projects for six months, Leininger's bosses instructed him to develop a computer. In February 1977, his prototype was shown to Charles Tandy, who, despite appearing unimpressed, gave it the go-ahead. (Apparently, Tandy had already leaked the story to the press.) Tandy agreed to build a cautious 3,500 units, one for each RadioShack store.

028_29

Manufacturer: Tandy RadioShack **Name:** TRS-80	**Launched:** August 1977 **Country of Origin:** USA

SPECIFICATION

CPU model: Z80
Speed: 1.77MHz
RAM: 4KB
Special features: Modified 12in black-and-white RCA TV used as display
Local price at launch: $399

COMPANY HISTORY

TRS stands for Tandy RadioShack. The two were originally separate companies. Tandy was formed by friends Norton Hinkley and Dave L. Tandy, who, after meeting by chance in 1919 in Fort Worth, Texas, decided to start the Hinkley-Tandy Leather Company.

After serving in the US Navy during World War II, Dave's son Charles D. Tandy returned to Fort Worth, but clashed with Hinkley. The company split, and father and son went into business together, in 1950, forming the Tandy Leather Company.

RadioShack was formed back in 1921 by brothers Theodore and Milton Deutschmann, who opened a store in Boston supplying equipment to ship-radio operators and ham enthusiasts. They named the company after the nautical term for the room above the ship's bridge, where the radio equipment was housed. By the early Sixties, RadioShack was established but falling on hard times. Charles Tandy, now chairman of his company and interested in electronics, saw the bankrupt chain as an opportunity for growth and snapped it up in 1963.

Tandy RadioShack TRS-80

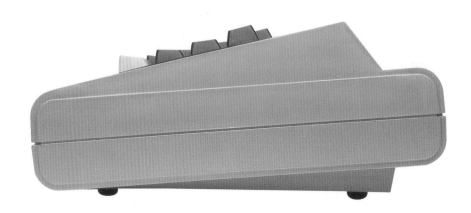

030_31

| Manufacturer: | Tandy RadioShack |
| Name: | TRS-80 |

WHAT HAPPENED NEXT

Initially priced at just $399, the TRS-80 cost much less than its immediate competitors the Commodore PET and Apple II, and within a month it had orders for over 10,000 units. Inevitably, its lower build quality earned it the nickname Trash 80, but sales continued to increase.

In 1979, the Model-II arrived, featuring a faster CPU and eight-inch disk drives. The Model-III followed in 1980, along with a new colour computer, affectionately known as the Coco. Later in 1984, the Model-1000 PC clone became Tandy's best-selling computer, signalling the end for the proprietary TRS-80.

The TRS-80's futuristic plastic housing contained a large heat sink to dissipate the warmth the machine generated. Besides heat, the computer generated enough radio interference to prevent users from listening while they worked.

digital : retro

INPUT/OUTPUT

1 Monitor

2 Cassette interface

3 Expansion port

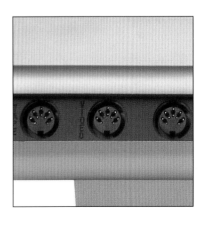

DID YOU KNOW?

In the UK, RadioShack stores were simply known as Tandy. Legend has it that "RadioShack" was already owned by an electronics shop on London's Finchley Road, which refused to sell its name. In 1999, UK mobile-phone retailer Carphone Warehouse bought all 270 of Tandy's UK outlets. Some stores became subsidiary Tecno Camera, which was later acquired by photographic retailer Jessops. Tandy may no longer be a household name in the UK, but the company remains a dominant force in the US, where, in 2000, it was renamed RadioShack Corporation. Today, an estimated 94% of all Americans live or work within five minutes of a RadioShack store or dealer, while 99% of American households visit one of the stores at least once every three years.

Nascom-1

Legend holds that the idea for the NASCOM-1 computer kit came to John Marshall while he chatted on a transatlantic flight. As in all good stories, he sketched it onto a napkin for future reference. Mirroring the successful marketing of the MITS Altair, the NASCOM kit would be sold through a magazine that would also publish features on assembly. The magazine was *Wireless World*.

Marshall subsequently commissioned Chris Shelton of Shelton Instruments in London to design the NASCO Microcomputer, or, as it later became known, the NASCOM-1. With a target price of £200 and a market of hobbyists, Shelton knew the NASCOM-1 would have to use existing domestic equipment where possible. Shelton approached digital television specialist Paul Johnson, who'd previously developed a VDU terminal that used a normal TV for a display. Johnson was contracted to develop the hardware, and later cofounded Tangerine (see Microtan 65 on p50).

The Z80 processor was chosen for the NASCOM-1, as several home applications had already been written for it, and MOSTEK proved to be very helpful during the development of the system. Two KB of RAM was fitted, half of which was devoted to video memory. Finally, a supplier of modestly priced QWERTY keyboards was found, although they still ended up being the single most expensive component in the system.

Manufacturer: NASCOM Microcomputers	**Launched:** November 1977
Model: NASCOM-1	**Country of Origin:** England

SPECIFICATION

CPU model: MOSTEK Z80
Speed: 2KB
RAM: 2KB
Special features: Full-size keyboard
Local price at launch: £197.50 kit-form

COMPANY HISTORY

NASCOM Microcomputers was set up by John Marshall in 1977 to sell a UK home-computer kit made up of components originally distributed from California-based North American Semiconductor Company, or NAS.

NAS operated two subsidiaries that distributed components to enthusiasts: Lynx Electronics in the US and NASCO in the UK, the latter run by John Marshall. Marshall had seen the high standard of computer clubs and fairs while visiting NAS in California and knew the UK market was also hungry for a computer kit. As luck would have it, NASCO already imported most of the components required for such a kit. All that was needed was someone to design it.

WHAT HAPPENED NEXT

Before launching the NASCOM-1, its technical director Tony Rundle asked Marshall how many units they needed to sell to break even. Marshall reckoned 200 units would turn a profit, but selling 400 would be great. They need not have worried. The NASCOM-1 sold 400 units in its first fortnight and exhausted the company's supply of cheap keyboards. Since alternatives cost almost as much as the entire NASCOM kit, the project was in trouble until Marshall discovered another supplier. An estimated 12,000 NASCOM-1s were sold through *Wireless World*.

The NASCOM-1's success resulted in the formation of a dedicated company, with Marshall as MD. Eighteen months later, the NASCOM-2 was launched, but after disappointing sales, NASCOM ran out of funding and called in the receivers. Marshall subsequently set up Gemini, while in 1981, the NASCOM name was sold to Lucas Logic, who launched the NASCOM-3 later that year.

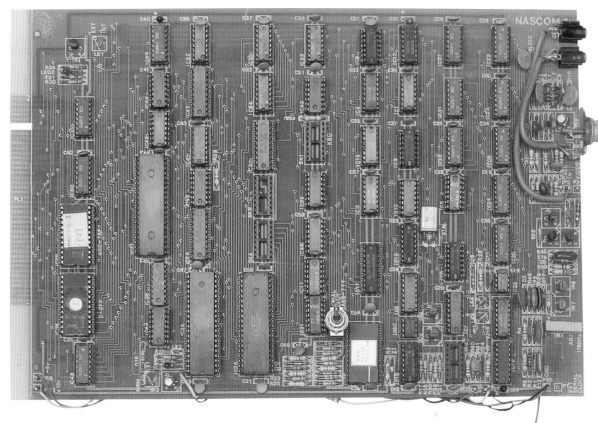

Sharp
MZ-80K

034_35

In 1971, Sharp produced the first 4-bit microprocessor, for use in a Coca-Cola point-of-sales terminal. This chip later became part of a computer kit for enthusiasts. Despite consisting of little more than a motherboard, numeric keypad, loudspeaker and four-digit LED display, demand for the kit turned out to be higher than expected, proving to Sharp that there was a market for personal computers.

Under the management of Kaoru Nakanishi, Sharp's Electronics Division began development of its own personal computer designed for the serious business market. During this time, the competitor that really caught Sharp's eye was the Commodore PET 2001. Commodore did, however, have one big advantage over rival computer manufacturers: it owned the 6502 processor and hence could deploy it at cost.

With its own semiconductor facilities, Sharp was understandably reluctant to buy in a third-party microprocessor, but the company equally lacked the time to create its own. Sharp's solution was to license an existing processor, striking a deal with Zilog to manufacture its Z80 chip – the only condition being that Sharp was unable to sell its own Z80 chips in the US.

Despite licensing a processor, Sharp could employ plenty of its own technologies too, including a tape deck and a ten-inch monitor. Both were fitted into an all-in-one design launched as the MZ-80K in December 1978, costing ¥198,000 in kit form.

Manufacturer: Sharp	**Launched:** December 1978
Model: MZ-80K	**Country of Origin:** Japan

SPECIFICATION

CPU model: Sharp Z80
Speed: 2MHz
RAM: 20KB
Special features: Built-in tape deck and 10in monitor
Local price at launch: ¥198,000 (Yen) kit-form

COMPANY HISTORY

The Sharp Corporation was founded in September 1912 by 19-year-old Tokuji Hayakawa, and later named after one of his inventions. Hayakawa had been working as an apprentice metalworker in Tokyo since 1902, when he was just nine years old. After seeing a movie featuring a character who wore a loose-fitting belt, Hayakawa was inspired to design a snap buckle, but he didn't expect many orders from a population that mostly wore kimonos. Western clothing soon grew in popularity, though, and demand for Hayakawa's buckle exploded. When Hayakawa was faced with an order for almost 5,000 buckles, his master granted him his blessing to set up his own company. Three years later, in 1915, Hayakawa used his metalworking expertise to develop the first mechanical pencil, later naming a refined version the Ever-Sharp Pencil. After the Great Kanto Earthquake of 1923, in which he lost both his family and business, Hayakawa relocated to Osaka, where he bought his first radio and realized electronics were Sharp's destiny.

1978

Sharp
MZ-80K

036_37

Manufacturer: Sharp
Model: MZ-80K

WHAT HAPPENED NEXT

The MZ-80K sold well in the regions that
Zilog's licensing allowed, including
Europe. It was also the first in a long line of
MZ computers from Sharp. These began
as enhanced versions of the original
model, but they later adopted the
IBM PC architecture.

INPUT/OUTPUT
1 Expansion bus

digital : retro

DID YOU KNOW?
Sharp was also responsible for a string of innovations, including the first Japanese TV in 1953, first microwave oven in 1961 and first transistor calculator in 1964. Today it's famous for many technologies, from home entertainment equipment and LCD panels to microwave ovens and solar power.

Sharp's "clean design" philosophy extended to the MZ-80K's internal as well as external workings. In practical terms, this meant that it contained no operating sys tem, so even BASIC had to be loaded from cassette. On the outside, though, the reflective surface of the keys made typing problematic.

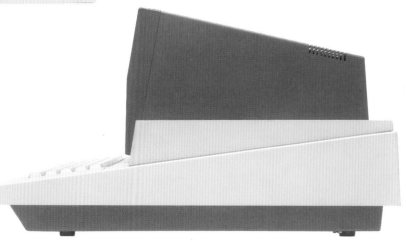

1979

Atari
400/800

During the summer of 1977, work began on the successor to the Atari VCS game console. The original VCS team, led by Steve Mayer, Ron Milner and Joe Decuir, started developing a custom chipset, but Atari's new boss Ray Kassar had different ideas.

Back in 1976, Nolan Bushnell had sold Atari to Warner Brothers, who later hired Kassar in 1978. Bushnell and Kassar clashed on the future direction of Atari, whereupon Bushnell left and Kassar became CEO. Atari management wanted a personal computer to compete with the likes of Apple, and refocused its engineers on this goal.

The next-generation game-console project evolved into two new computers sharing the same custom chipset, but packaged in different ways. The Atari 400 was a game machine that could do just enough keyboarding to handle complex input for titles like *Star Raiders*, while the 800 was a personal computer that happened to play the same games.

Revealing their original parentage, both computers offered excellent gaming facilities including four joystick ports, hardware sprites, four voice sounds and slots for either one or two cartridges (400 and 800 respectively). The main difference between them was memory and keyboard. Designed as a budget machine for children, the 400 (pictured) had a membrane keyboard and 8KB RAM, while the more serious 800 featured a full-travel keyboard and 16KB RAM.

038_39

Manufacturer: Atari	**Launched:** January 1979
Model: 400 (pictured) / 800	**Country of Origin:** USA

SPECIFICATION

CPU model: 6502
Speed: 1.8MHz
RAM: 8KB (400), 16KB (800)
Special features: Four joystick ports, custom chips with sprite capabilities, membrane keyboard on 400 model
Local price at launch: $499 (400), $899 (800)

COMPANY HISTORY

See Atari VCS, p24

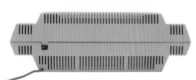

Atari
400/800

Manufacturer: Atari
Model: 400 (pictured) / 800

DID YOU KNOW?

The Atari 400 and 800 were code-named Candy and Colleen after female administrative assistants at Atari. According to Joe Decuir, Atari's marketing team thought they were merely continuing a trend of female code names that had started with the earlier VCS – but the Stella was actually named after Decuir's bicycle. The trio of custom chips featured in the 400 and 800 were called ANTIC, CTIA and POKEY, dedicated to DMA addressing, video data and I/O, respectively.

The Atari 400's biggest drawback, the membrane keyboard, prompted the market to provide a number of replacements. These either connected to one of the ports via a cable, or required you to open the case and replace the supplied part. One was even adhesive, placed atop the original keyboard: the replacement keys simply pressed down on those beneath them.

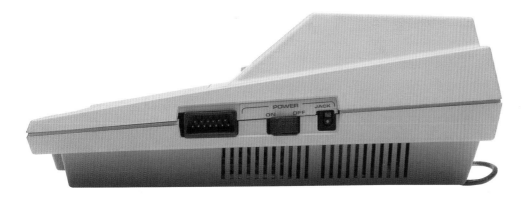

INPUT/OUTPUT (400)
1 RF TV
2 Cartridge slot
3 Expansion bus
4 Atari Serial I/O (SIO)
5 4x joystick ports
6 Tape recorder

INPUT/OUTPUT (800)
1 RGB and Composite video
2 2x cartridge slots
3 Expansion bus
4 Atari Serial I/O (SIO)
5 4x joystick ports
6 Tape recorder
7 4x internal slots

WHAT HAPPENED NEXT

The Atari 400 and 800 were launched at the January 1979 Consumer Electronics Show and were sold until 1983, by which time both had more memory and new graphics chipsets. In 1982, Atari launched the 1200XL, but technical problems resulted in many buyers sticking with the older 800. Later, the 600XL and 800XL (pictured below) arrived. These were essentially versions of the original 400 and 800, but including expansion-slot options earlier FCC regulations had prevented. In summer 1984, Atari was sold to former Commodore boss Jack Tramiel, who cancelled the XL platform for the XE (XL line Enhanced) range. The newly developed 16-bit ST range followed in January 1985.

Texas Instruments TI-99/4

In 1952, Texas Instruments entered the semiconductor business, opening a research division the following year and producing the first commercial transistor radio one year later. In 1958, Jack Kilby joined TI and invented the first integrated circuit. By the Seventies, TI was a world-leader in semiconductors and enjoyed a roaring calculator business.

Then in 1975, TI launched the TMS 9900, the first 16-bit micro-processor. It may have been way ahead of its time, but it found itself only employed in TI's own 990/4 and 990/5 mini-computers, both of which were too expensive to attract third party developers.

Computers were of course the perfect vehicle for selling TI's own components, so it decided to join the emerging micro-computer market and develop three affordable systems for the home, business and professional markets; TI's management insisted all use the TMS 9900 processor.

Later the business and professional projects were dropped in favour of concentrating on the home computer. TI's engineers equipped it with the TMS 9900 processor clocked at 3MHz and fitted 16KB RAM. TI's strategy would be to sell it cheaply, while making money on the software. It subsequently launched the TI-99/4 in June 1979.

042_43

Manufacturer: Texas Instruments	**Launched:** June 1979
Model: TI-99/4	**Country of Origin:** USA

SPECIFICATION

CPU model: TMS 9900
Speed: 3MHz
RAM: 16KB
Special features: Chicklet calculator-style keyboard, Texas Instruments CPU
Local price at launch: $1150

COMPANY HISTORY

Texas Instruments was founded on 16 May 1930 by Eugene McDermott and John Clarence "Doc" Karcher. Originally known as the Geophysical Service and headquartered in Dallas, Texas, it specialized in oil exploration using seismographic equipment of its own design. In 1939 it changed names to Coronado Corporation, but kept Geophysical Service Incorporated (GSI) as a subsidiary.

During early December 1941, GSI employee John Erik Jonsson learned Coronado was being sold and was asked if he wanted to buy the geophysical side of the business. Fearing they might otherwise be out of jobs, Jonsson and Eugene McDermott, along with former employees Cecil Green and HB Peacock, raised funds and bought GSI, becoming owners on 6th December 1941: the eve of the Pearl Harbor attacks.

GSI adapted its technology for the US Navy to locate enemy submarines during the war, and later grew, widening its product range. To reflect these changes, GSI was renamed General Instruments Incorporated in January 1951, but after confusion with another company, changed again to Texas Instruments.

1979

Texas Instruments TI-99/4

044_45

Manufacturer: Texas Instruments
Model: TI-99/4

INPUT/OUTPUT
1 Tape interface
2 RGB video (non-FCC)
3 2x joystick
4 Cartridge slot

WHAT HAPPENED NEXT

TI had originally intended for the 99/4 to exploit a TV as a cheap display, but its RF modulator failed FCC tests, forcing the company to bundle an expensive monitor instead. What began as a budget proposition now cost $1150.

Its chicklet keyboard, while fine for calculators, was also unpopular. Worse, whether by accident or design, TI had made it virtually impossible for anyone other than

itself and official licensees to develop peripherals or software for the TI-99/4. Taking these criticisms on board, TI launched the superior TI-99/4A model (as pictured on p43) in June 1981 with improved keyboard and a lower price of $525, albeit without monitor. While the 99/4A was very successful, it entered into an aggressive price war with Commodore, resulting in TI pulling out of home computers in October 1983.

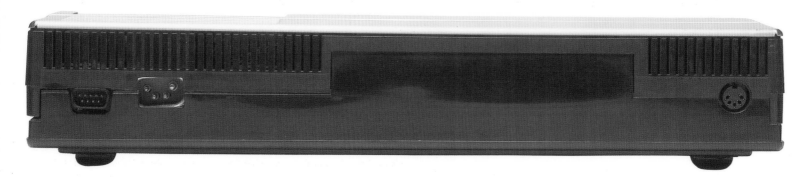

DID YOU KNOW?

On 11th June 1978, Texas Instruments announced a new speech synthesis chip. TI combined this with a pair of 128KB ROMs and a special version of the TMS 1000 "micro-computer-on-a-chip" to serve as the electronics behind its new Speak and Spell toy. Announced on the same day as the synthesis chip, Speak and Spell was designed to help children spell and pronounce over 200 commonly mis-spelt words. It was the first time solid-state circuitry had been used to reproduce the human voice in a consumer product. Speak and Spell cost $50 when it became available later in the summer of 1978.

In 1977, two years after the Handlers left Mattel, the company decided it should enter the games market. Richard Chang, Mattel's head of Design and Development, found almost everything he needed in a General Instruments (GI) integrated circuit catalogue.

Chang's eye was caught by a video game system called the Gimini 6900, consisting of standard GI components. He contacted GI, and worked with them to enhance the graphics, while APh Technology Consultants in Pasadena was hired to write the operating system. Dave James, an artist from Mattel, worked with APh to define the graphics, including the console's famous running man.

Mattel's directors, however, got cold feet and put the project on hold, leaving Chang and APh to concentrate on developing new handheld electronic games. By the time 1979 came round, though, the video game market was sufficiently strong to allow Mattel executive Jeff Rochlis to convince the board to resurrect the console project.

The hardware team, lead by Dave Chandler, completed the system and created the curious hand controllers that shunned joysticks in favour of a flat-disc, while David Rolfe at APh finished the software, including the Exec OS and *Major League Baseball*, the console's first game. After a successful test period in Gottschalk's department stores around Fresno during late 1979, the IntelliVision Master Component System was widely launched early the following year.

Mattel IntelliVision

Manufacturer: Mattel
Model: IntelliVision

Launched: November 1979
Country of Origin: USA

COMPANY HISTORY

Mattel was founded in 1945 by Ruth and Elliot Handler and Harold "Matt" Matson out of a garage workshop in Southern California; the company name was derived from combining Matt and Elliot. The company started out producing picture frames, but soon developed a popular sideline in doll house furniture made from scraps. Matson later sold his share to the Handlers who, encouraged by the success of the doll furniture, subsequently concentrated on toys.

In 1955, Mattel began advertising toys on the *Mickey Mouse Club* show, but the company's defining moment came in 1959 when, inspired by her daughter Barbara playing with cut-out paper figures, Ruth Handler suggested producing a girl's doll. The doll was christened after her daughter's nickname, Barbie, with Ken (named for the Handlers' son) arriving in 1961, followed by friend Midge in 1963 and sister Skipper in 1965. Mattel's second major brand, Hot Wheels, rolled out in 1968.

SPECIFICATION

CPU model: General Instruments 1610
Speed: 1MHz
RAM: 2KB
Special features: Hand controllers with flat discs instead of joysticks
Local price at launch: $299

Mattel
IntelliVision

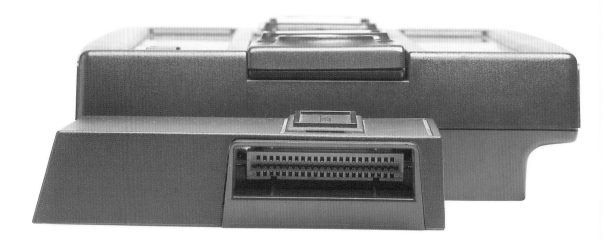

048_49

Manufacturer: Mattel
Model: IntelliVision

WHAT HAPPENED NEXT

The IntelliVision's 159 x 96 pixel graphics were absolutely staggering in 1980, and made the rival Atari VCS look primitive in comparison. Mattel's advertising repeatedly pointed this out, but fearing its in-house programmers would be poached by Atari, kept their identities secret. A magazine article referred to them as The Blue Sky Rangers, a nickname which

stuck at Mattel. Several add-ons were launched, including a voice module and a new Mark II console in 1983, but by this time the video games market was in trouble, and Mattel soon closed the doors on all its non-toy divisions. While it really was game over for the IntelliVision at Mattel in January 1984, 3 million units had already been sold.

Like the Atari VCS before it, the IntelliVision's design owed more than a little to the music centre, featuring a woodgrain plastic strip. This fitted in with the family-friendly marketing campaign that placed the console in the living room.

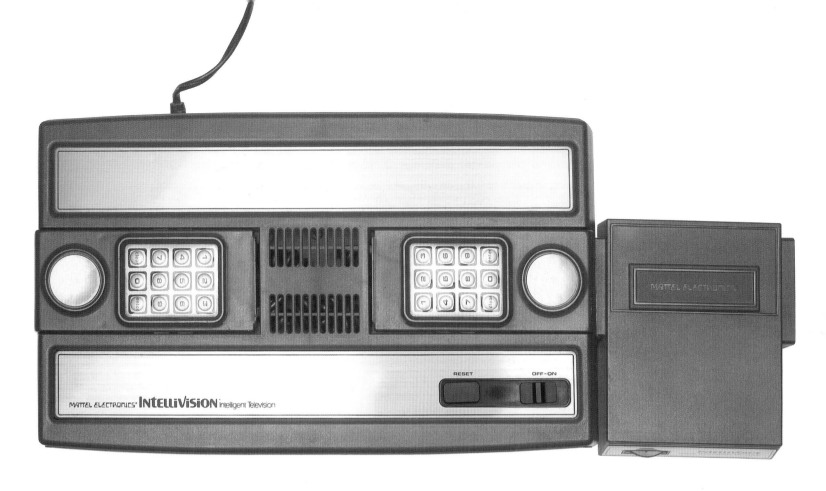

The game controllers could be stowed in the console, with their attached coiled cables tidily concealed. When in use, an overlay could be placed over the keypad to highlight the buttons' functions in the game.

DID YOU KNOW?
Mattel promised a keyboard add-on unit for the IntelliVision which would turn it into a computer from day one, but high costs saw it constantly delayed. Indeed, during his speech at the 1981 Mattel Electronics Christmas Party, comedian Jay Leno even joked the world's three big lies were "The check is in the mail, I'll still respect you in the morning and the Keyboard will be out in the spring."

Somewhat more seriously though, the keyboard's non-arrival resulted in Mattel being investigated for fraud, and in mid-1982 was ordered by the FTC to pay a reputed monthly fine of $10,000 until the promised peripheral was widely available. Mattel quickly produced a keyboard to placate a handful of its most disgruntled customers, but then set to work on an actual home computer, the ill-fated Aquarius (see p126).

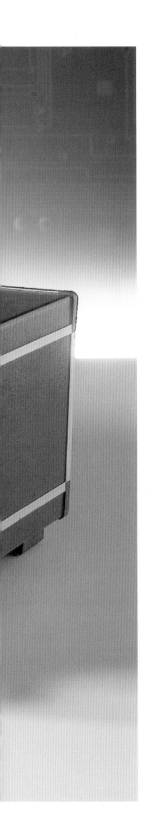

While still working at Cambridge Consultants, Johnson developed a new computer in his spare time that used a TV for its monitor. Chatting in the Cambridge Consultants drawing office, Johnson claimed that with £10,000 backing he could make a fortune. Barry Muncaster, a contractor at the time, overheard Johnson's claims, followed him back to his office and asked if he really meant it.

Subsequently convinced by Johnson's plan, Muncaster found an investor who helpfully also offered them warehouse space on their Cambridgeshire grounds. After buying out the company name from Johnson's school friend for a few hundred pounds, they registered Tangerine Computer Systems and started work on building Johnson's system.

The 6502 processor was chosen due to its popularity in other systems like the Apple II and Commodore PET. Johnson noticed the 6502 also only accessed its memory half the time, leaving it effectively free for the other half. He exploited this by using the memory's idle period to drive the display, thereby reducing component costs.

The Microtan name was formed from the words Microprocessor and Tangerine, while 65 was tagged on in reference to its processor. The Microtan 65 was launched at the end of 1979 for £69+VAT in kit-form, although a ready-built option was offered later for £79+VAT.

Tangerine Microtan 65

Manufacturer: Tangerine Computer Systems
Name: Microtan 65

Launched: December 1979
Country of Origin: England

COMPANY HISTORY

Tangerine Computer Systems was set up by Dr Paul Johnson and Barry Muncaster near Cambridge, England in October 1979. Johnson had previously graduated from Bradford University with a degree in digital audio and a PhD in electronics related to digital television.

At this time microprocessor evaluation kits required ungainly 110 Teletype boards, so with his specialization Johnson developed a VDU Terminal that could be used with a normal TV set. On the strength of this, Johnson was approached to work on the NASCOM-1 *(see p32)*.

Johnson joined Cambridge Consultants after leaving university, but started a new company in his spare time with an old school friend. Following the trend for fruity company names they called themselves Tangerine and produced a kit-form VDU terminal for evaluating microprocessors. After meeting Muncaster – see system story – they bought the name from Johnson's school friend and officially registered the company as Tangerine Computer Systems.

SPECIFICATION

CPU model: 6502
Speed: 1MHz
RAM: 1KB
Special features: TV output, memory shared with video
Local price at launch: £69+VAT kit-form

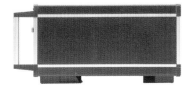

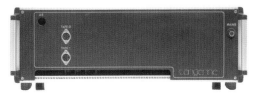

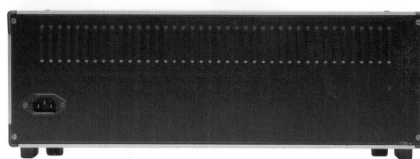

Tangerine
Microtan
65

Manufacturer: Tangerine
Computer Systems
Name: Microtan 65

Unlike the emerging consumer systems, the Microtan was very much an enthusiasts' machine with a scientific-looking box. The basic ROM contained not an operating system but a "monitor program" called TANBUG.

WHAT HAPPENED NEXT

The success of the Microtan 65 saw Johnson quit Cambridge Consultants in January 1980 to join Tangerine full-time. That same year the Prestel service was launched by BT to encourage telephone usage, and Tangerine used some of the Microtan architecture to create its Tantel Prestel adapter the following year. The Tantel housed a microcomputer, modem and Teletext display for £170, which was impressive considering dedicated modems of the day could cost over £1000. During 1981, Tangerine also developed the Z80-based Tiger, which was sold to a company called HH for further funding. Tangerine later formed Oric Products International, launching the Oric-1 in 1983 *(see p122)*.

INPUT/OUTPUT

1 Bus
2 Tape (300/2400 baud)

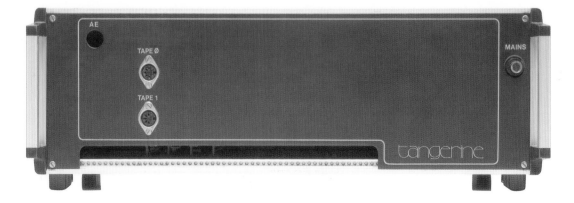

digital : retro

DID YOU KNOW?
The Microtan 65's price of just £69+VAT in kit-form may have been very affordable, but you only got a hexadecimal keyboard with it; a full QWERTY keyboard cost extra.

One advanced feature of the Microtan (for its age) was that it was able to produce a flicker-free display. It took advantage of the 6502 processor's regular internal cycle (where no calls on external memory are made), meaning that the external memory is available for the video controller at regular intervals.

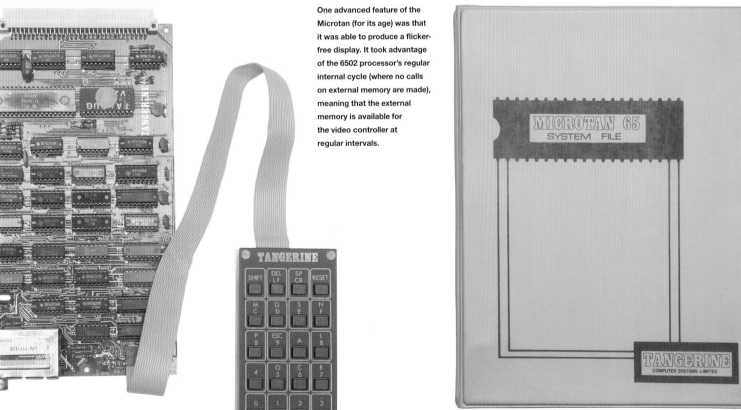

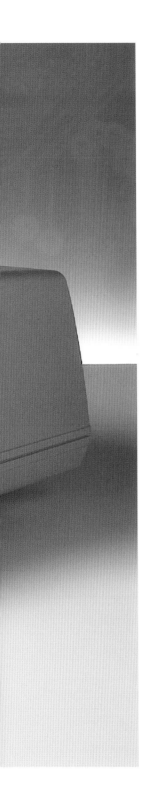

As HP grew, it was responsible for a number of world firsts including the 9100A scientific desktop calculator in 1968, the HP-35 handheld scientific calculator in 1972 and the HP-65 programmable pocket calculator in 1974. These were born out of HP's Advanced Products Division (APD), which in 1973 employed Steve Wozniak after he dropped out of Berkeley; Wozniak later formed Apple with Steve Jobs. Shortly before relocating to Corvallis, Oregon in 1976, APD began working on its most sophisticated calculator project yet, code-named Capricorn. Every single aspect was designed from scratch by a team of APD veterans including Kent Henscheid, Nelson Mills and Tim Williams.

Rather than employing a third-party processor, the Capricorn team actually developed a brand-new CPU sporting a unique architecture. The chip may have technically been an 8-bit design, but by accessing eight registers simultaneously could actually work on 64 bits of information at once. Unlike other processors, which worked in binary alone, the Capricorn's chip could additionally operate with Binary Coded Decimal, which gave it an unprecedented arithmetic accuracy of 12 digits.

The Capricorn system also featured a built-in 5in monitor, tape drive and thermal printer. It ran entirely silently, without a single fan, but in order to achieve this only one peripheral could operate at a time. Consequently the display and tape drive had to be temporarily powered-off when printing.

Manufacturer: Hewlett Packard
Model: HP-85

Launched: January 1980
Country of Origin: USA

COMPANY HISTORY

Hewlett Packard was founded on 1st January 1939 by Bill Hewlett and Dave Packard, who decided which name would go first by the toss of a coin. Bill and Dave were classmates at Stanford University, graduating as electrical engineers in 1934. Upon returning from holiday in the Colorado mountains, Bill continued studying at MIT while Dave took a job with General Electric.
Having become good friends on the trip though, they decided to start a business together. Dave and his wife moved into a flat at 367 Addison Avenue, Palo Alto, California, while Bill rented a cottage nearby. With $538 in capital the pair set to work in Dave's garage. Their first product was the HP200A audio oscillator, used to test sound equipment; Dave later admitted the model number was chosen to make it sound like they'd been around a while. With Hewlett Packard officially formalized, Walt Disney was one of its first major customers, ordering eight model 200Bs for testing audio equipment used in the presentation of *Fantasia*. HP moved out of the garage in 1940.

SPECIFICATION

CPU model: Custom HP design
Speed: 613KHz
RAM: 16KB
Special features: Built-in keyboard, 5in CRT monitor, thermal printer and tape drive. Silent fanless operation
Local price at launch: $3250

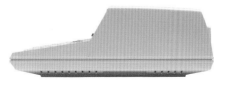

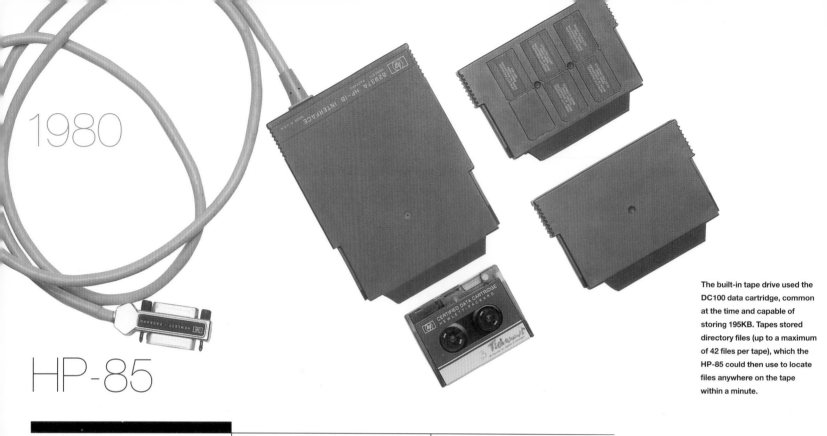

HP-85

056_57

The built-in tape drive used the DC100 data cartridge, common at the time and capable of storing 195KB. Tapes stored directory files (up to a maximum of 42 files per tape), which the HP-85 could then use to locate files anywhere on the tape within a minute.

Manufacturer: Hewlett Packard
Model: HP-85

WHAT HAPPENED NEXT

Capricorn took four years to develop, eventually being launched in January 1980 for $3250. Officially called the HP-85, it uniquely offered the best of two worlds: with its 12-digit accuracy many considered it the ultimate programmable calculator, but with programmable basic and, later, assembly language options, it could also operate as a powerful microcomputer. The Series-80 range continued throughout the Eighties with several enhanced models until, like most other companies, HP adopted the increasingly dominant IBM PC architecture.

INPUT/OUTPUT
1 4x proprietory I/O port
2 Cartridge slot

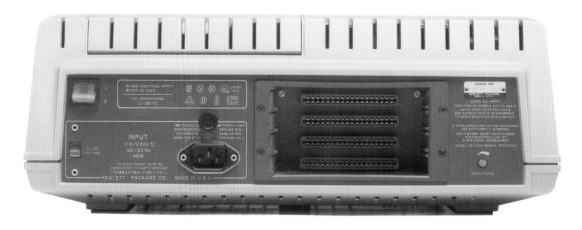

The HP-85 was designed to fit into an office environment, and as such has much in common with Hewlett Packard's range of desktop calculators. A padded carrying case with a distinctly military appearance was also available

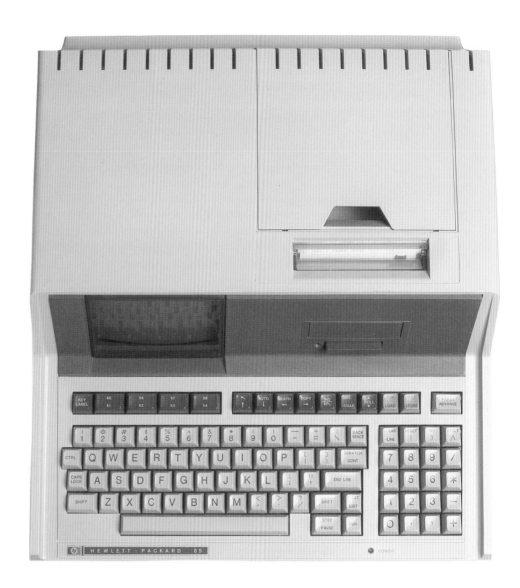

DID YOU KNOW?

HP's Advanced Products Division encouraged its employees to pursue their own projects on approval and even supplied components. Like several others in the division, Steve Wozniak was working on a computer project. He based it on the new 6502 processor that Chuck Peddle was selling at a San Francisco computer fair for just $20. Wozniak's machine was finished in November 1975 and informally demonstrated to an HP supervisor in January 1976. The supervisor was impressed but explained APD couldn't take on any significant projects during its move to Corvallis, Oregon. Wozniak was allowed to keep his technology, though, which was later refined and launched as the Apple I.

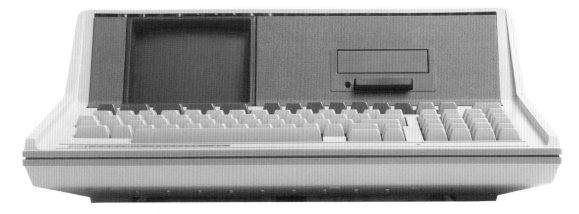

Sinclair ZX80

In summer 1978, Sinclair Radionics began work on a new computer funded by the UK government's National Enterprise Board (NEB). By May the following year, though, NEB announced plans to sell off Radionics' calculator and TV interests, which included the half-completed computer. This machine later became the Newbrain *(see p102)*.

Clive Sinclair himself resigned with a golden handshake and concentrated on a new computer project at his Science of Cambridge company. Jim Westwood, who'd joined Radionics in 1963, developed the hardware. Westwood had built a computer in his spare time in 1973 using an abandoned Radionics project, and later adapted it to use the Z80 processor. His familiarity with it made it a natural choice for the new machine.

Wanting to sell a computer to the man on the street, Sinclair was fanatical about meeting a low price point. To that end, Westwood's machine used the Z80, rather than an expensive video controller, to drive the screen. John Pemberton's tiny case design featured a membrane keyboard and low-cost vacuum forming.

Without in-house software expertise, Sinclair approached John Grant of Nine-Tiles to write the code. Single key-presses automatically generated entire words, both to reduce syntax errors by non-typists and to save on memory – an idea implemented on subsequent ZX models. Sinclair met his price point and launched the ZX80, named after its processor and year of introduction.

058_59

Manufacturer: Sinclair	**Launched:** January 1980
Model: ZX80	**Country of Origin:** England

SPECIFICATION

CPU model: Z80A
Speed: 3.25MHz
RAM: 1KB
Special features: Membrane keyboard, single-key word entry
Local price at launch: £79.99 (kit-form), £99.99 (ready-built)

COMPANY HISTORY

Clive Sinclair founded his first company, Radionics, on the 25th July 1961, less than a week before his 21st birthday. After completing his S-Levels four years earlier, Sinclair became editorial assistant at *Practical Wireless* magazine. Shortly after joining, though, the editor fell ill, retired and was soon followed by his assistant – leaving Sinclair to manage the title single-handedly.

The following year, while manning a stall at London's Olympia exhibition hall, Sinclair was approached by publisher Bernard Babani to become the editor of his electronics book company. Three years later, in 1961, Sinclair left to form Radionics, but he was forced to join another electronics magazine to raise funds when his backer withdrew. Radionics' first commercial product, the Sinclair Micro Amplifier, arrived toward the end of 1962, costing 28s/6d in old English money (or £3.42 today). Sinclair was subsequently responsible for the first pocket calculator and pocket television, while his first computer, the MK-14 kit, launched in 1977 and sold 50,000 units.

1980

Sinclair ZX80

060_61

Manufacturer: Sinclair	
Model: ZX80	

WHAT HAPPENED NEXT

Costing just £99.99, the ready-made ZX80 met Clive Sinclair's goal of delivering an affordable consumer computer and set the scene for the budget UK home-computer market. While not achieving the sales volumes of its follow-ups, the ZX80 still sold over 100,000 units during its lifespan. The ZX80 may have been remarkable for its price, but it wasn't without problems. To help meet Sinclair's budget, Westwood got the main processor to drive the display – but as a result, the screen flickered annoyingly. This and a lack of floating point mathematics were both addressed in the ZX81 follow-up, which, remarkably, managed to be cheaper still.

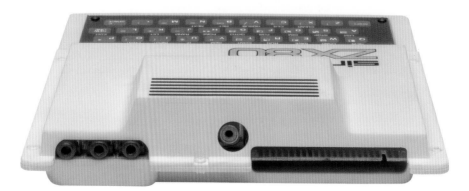

INPUT/OUTPUT

1 Tape
2 TV/RF video
3 ZX80 bus

Low cost drove the ZX80's design, although it should be known that Sinclair himself was equally fanatical about miniaturization as meeting specific price points. Measuring just 219 x 175 x 40mm, the ZX80 introduced the world to Sinclair's concept of seriously compact computers.

DID YOU KNOW?

Many of those who worked with Sinclair recall how the ZX80's design was driven by price, its capabilities a second priority. At one point, shortly before launch, Jim Westwood expressed concern that describing the ZX80 as a computer could be misleading, as its limited ROM hadn't allowed floating point mathematics capabilities. Sinclair replied that that wasn't the point: The ZX80 was designed to meet a strict price point and allow more people to learn about computing. That said, floating point capabilities were high on the list for the ZX81.

After launching the Acorn System 1, the team at Cambridge Processor Unit (CPU) intended to build a rack-mounted system designed for the educational and industrial markets. CPU co-founder Chris Curry, however, had something different in mind. While working with Sinclair, he'd seen the massive growth in the enthusiast market and believed they could tap this market by essentially fitting a System-1 computer into a friendly, consumer-styled case.

The new machine's specifications were subsequently discussed by the CPU team at the same picnic meeting where the name Acorn was coined. Like the System-1, it was to use a 6502 processor, running at 1MHz. Aiming for a low price point, the Acorn team expected to fit a membrane-style keyboard, but Curry found an affordable alternative based on touching gold-plate wires. Curry's friend Alan Boothroyd then designed a case around the new keyboard. Finally, Curry had a decent-quality photo taken to ensure that Acorn's ads looked obviously superior to those of its competitors.

Inspired by their physics backgrounds, the team christened the new machine the Atom and launched it in March 1980 in two versions – as a kit for £120, and preassembled for £170.

Acorn Atom

Manufacturer: Acorn Computers Ltd	**Launched:** March 1980
Model: Atom	**Country of Origin:** England

COMPANY HISTORY

Acorn was founded in December 1978 by Hermann Hauser and Chris Curry in Cambridge, England, although the company started life as Cambridge Processor Unit – CPU for short. Hauser had been a postdoctoral student at Cambridge University, while Curry had worked for Clive Sinclair's Science of Cambridge company for thirteen years. The pair had long been friends and were keen to work together.

After Hauser and Curry set up CPU, they were joined by former Cambridge lab assistant Chris Turner. In the early days, CPU operated out of one of Science of Cambridge's spare rooms and worked on new electronics for slot machines. Hauser then approached Cambridge undergraduate Sophie Wilson, whom he knew through Cambridge University's Processor Group (CUPG), to help him design an electronic pocket address book. Wilson suggested adapting one of her existing 6502-based designs, and an impressed Hauser asked her to build that instead. Wilson's machine became the System 1, launched as a kit in April 1979 under the new Acorn brand.

The name Acorn was coined at a company picnic at Curry's farmhouse. Hauser had suggested Intelligence Limited, but Acorn was chosen to suggest a growing company.

SPECIFICATION

CPU model: 6502
Speed: 1MHz
RAM: 2KB
Special features: High resolution 256 x 192 graphics
Local price at launch: £120 (kit-form), £170 (ready built)

Acorn
Atom

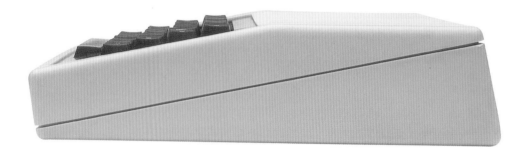

064_65

Manufacturer: Acorn Computers Ltd
Model: Atom

WHAT HAPPENED NEXT

The combination of decent hardware, Sophie Wilson's BASIC, an attractive case and superior advertising paid off. Hauser estimates that 10,000 Atoms sold over its span. The Atom was certainly impressive for its day, although it had build-quality issues: On some units, certain chips fitted below the keyboard were actually known to fall out of their sockets.

Acorn later created a successor, code-named the Proton. An early model impressed BBC engineers sufficiently to win Acorn the contract to adapt it into the legendary BBC Micro.

INPUT/OUTPUT
1 Acorn bus extension
2 Tape interface
3 UHF (modulated) TV

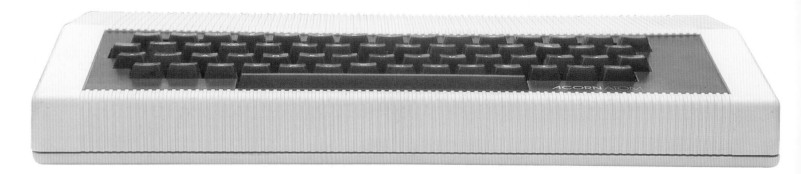

DID YOU KNOW?

The Atom was based on Wilson's System-1, but instead of using its 6845 processor and multiple cards to generate video output, Nick Toop, a former colleague of Curry's, suggested that the Atom employ the new integrated 6847 graphics chip instead. The 6847 may have been a convenient all-in-one solution, but it generated a colour NTSC signal designed for US-based TVs. Toop, however, discovered UK PAL TV sets were able to lock onto the signal, albeit only in monochrome. That said, for its low price point, the Atom did boast an impressively high resolution of 256 x 192.

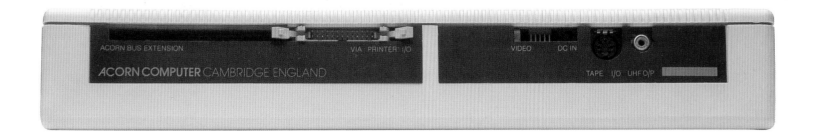

ACORN BUS EXTENSION   VIA PRINTER I/O   VIDEO   DC IN   TAPE I/O UHF O/P

ACORN COMPUTER CAMBRIDGE ENGLAND

Commodore
VIC-20

After launching the highly successful PET, Commodore boss Jack Tramiel grew keen to preempt the launch of any Japanese home computers. During a management meeting near London in early April 1980, Tramiel insisted Commodore enter the consumer market. Upon returning to the US, Commodore marketing strategist Michael Tomczyk prepared a thirty-page memo detailing the production and features of a possible consumer machine, and was put in charge of product management.

Albert Charpentier of Commodore's semiconductor division had developed a graphics component called the Video Interface Chip (VIC), intended for gaming systems. When the video-game market collapsed, though, the team considered other uses for it. Knowing Tramiel was interested in low-cost computers, new recruit Bob Yannes built a prototype that married the VIC with Commodore's 6502 processor.

Impressed by its potential, Tramiel took Yannes's prototype to Chuck Peddle's team, where Bill Seiler was already working on a low-cost computer project. Seiler was given one month to develop his and Yannes' ideas into a model in time for June's Consumer Electronics Show. The software was written by John Feagans's group, while much of the firmware was undertaken by Yashi Terakura in Japan. The machine was named VIC after its Video Interface Chip but, believing it sounded like a truck driver, Tomczyk suggested adding the number 20 – simply because it sounded friendly.

Manufacturer: Commodore	**Launched:** January 1981
Model: VIC-20	**Country of Origin:** USA

SPECIFICATION

CPU model: 6502A
Speed: 1MHz
RAM: 3.5KB
Special features: Full-size keyboard, required dedicated tape deck
Local price at launch: $299

COMPANY HISTORY

See **Commodore PET 2001, p016**

digital : retro

1981

Commodore VIC-20

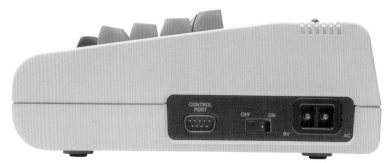

068_69

Manufacturer: Commodore
Model: VIC-20

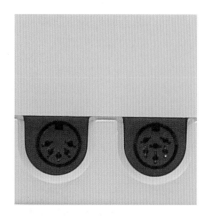

INPUT/OUTPUT
1 Joystick port
2 User port
3 Serial port
4 Cartridge port
5 RGB output
6 Tape interface

WHAT HAPPENED NEXT

The VIC-20 was first introduced in Japan as the VIC-1001 in September 1980, before being officially launched in the US the following January.

As the first colour computer to break $300, the VIC-20 was a very popular machine. Over its four-year lifespan, it sold more than 2.5 million units, with production reaching 9,000 units a day at its peak. In order to stay ahead of the Japanese, Commodore followed the VIC-20 with a far superior system just one year after the original launch. The Commodore 64 would later become be the best-selling computer of all time.

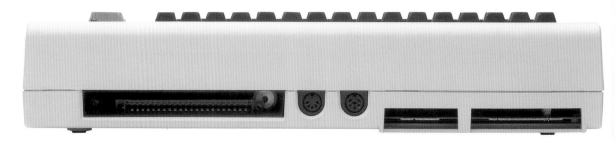

digital : retro

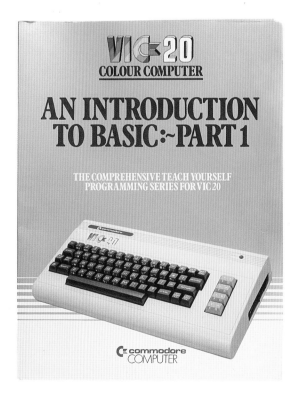

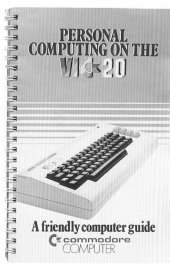

DID YOU KNOW?

Michael Tomczyk originally wanted to call the VIC-20 the Commodore Spirit. At the last minute, though, he was informed by Japanese colleagues that they didn't have "friendly ghosts" in Japan, where his proposed name would end up sounding like the Commodore Ghoul or Commodore Zombie. The name was scrapped and VIC was chosen instead. The model introduced in Japan was called the VIC-1001, as a respectful nod to the movie *2001*.

1981

Sinclair ZX81

The Sinclair ZX80 may have been the first computer to break the UK's significant £100 price point, but Clive Sinclair was determined to make its successor even cheaper. After Jim Westwood made improvements, including eliminating the ZX80's infamous screen-flicker, Sinclair himself looked into ways to reduce costs.

His solution was to exploit new manufacturing techniques that allowed many chips to be integrated into a single component that was cheaper to produce and install. Ultimately, eighteen of the ZX80's twenty-one chips were integrated into a single custom Uncommitted Logic Array (ULA), produced by Ferranti. This allowed the new ZX81 to be built with just four chips: the Z80 processor, the custom ULA and one each for the ROM and RAM.

John Grant's Nine Tiles company was once again commissioned to write the software, adapted from the original ZX80 code. The ROM size had, however, doubled from 4KB to 8KB, allowing new recruit Steve Vickers to add floating point arithmetic and additional BASIC features.

Rick Dickinson designed a new case and, while a membrane keyboard was again employed for cost reasons, the budget did this time stretch to include injection moulding. The ZX81, named after its year of introduction, was launched that March as a kit or ready assembled.

070_71

Manufacturer: Sinclair	**Launched:** March 1981
Model: ZX81	**Country of Origin:** England

SPECIFICATION

CPU model: Z80A
Speed: 3.25MHz
RAM: 1KB
Special features: Membrane keyboard, optional 16KB RamPak
Local price at launch: £49.95 (kit-form), £69.95 (ready-built)

COMPANY HISTORY

See **Sinclair ZX80, p60**

digital : retro

Sinclair ZX81

Manufacturer: Sinclair
Model: ZX81

Among the extra features afforded by doubling the 4KB of ROM in the original ZX80 were instructions to control a printer add-on. This, like many of the ZX81's peripherals, came in matching black ABS plastic, regarded at the time as much more aesthetically pleasing than its predecessor.

WHAT HAPPENED NEXT

Sinclair initially sold the ZX81 via mail order, but it made a deal with UK newsstand chain W H Smith to sell it in its retail stores, which resulted in over 350,000 units sold in its first year. The ZX81 was a huge commercial success, but it did have problems, which famously included a bug in its square-root calculations.

Probably most infuriating of all, though, was the optional 16KB RamPak, which could crash the system at the slightest provocation. The ZX Printer may also have been affordable at just £49.95, but its narrow, aluminum-coated output was famously described as "a rather evil-looking toilet roll". That said, the ZX81 arguably kick-started the home-computer boom in the UK – not to mention abroad – and set the scene for its successor to become one of the best-selling machines of all time.

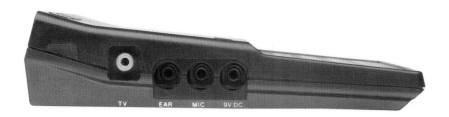

DID YOU KNOW?

After taking over manufacture of the earlier ZX80, US company Timex was again contracted by Sinclair to produce the new ZX81 at its Dundee factory in Scotland. When the ZX81 was launched in the UK, though, a considerable number were being exported to the US. Sinclair subsequently used its relationship with Timex to sell the ZX81, rebranded as the TS-1000, in the US. A new version of the ZX81, with a built-in RamPak fitted into a ZX Spectrum case, was also sold exclusively in the US as the TS-1500. This model proved less successful, however.

One of the chief problems with the ZX80 was that it needed to turn the display off while performing calculations, resulting in an infuriating flicker. In the ZX81, this was still the case in "fast" mode, but a "slow" mode was added, which – like other computers – continued to refresh the screen during calculation.

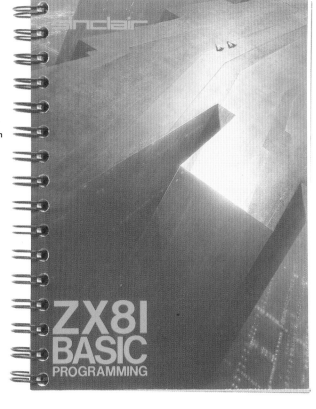

Technical book publisher Adam Osborne long believed that a genuinely useful computer should travel with its owner. The story goes that he was inspired by a visit to the legendary Xerox Palo Alto Research Center in 1980, where he saw the portable Notetaker machine. Whether or not this is true, Osborne set to work on his own portable computer, entirely funded by his $250,000 sale of Osborne Books to McGraw Hill the previous year.

At the 1980 West Coast Computer Fair, Osborne spotted Lee Felsenstein, a circuit-board designer who'd reviewed some of his books, and they discussed starting a company. After asking Felsenstein to propose several products, Osborne announced what they were really going to produce: he sketched a crude side view of a machine propped up by a fold-down keyboard. The machine would also have to fit under an airline seat.

Felsenstein designed the electronics, creating a system that featured two five-and-a-quarter-inch disc drives and a five-inch monitor. With the fold-down keyboard doubling as a lid, the system measured 20 x 14 x 8 inches and weighed in at twenty-four pounds: unparalleled portability for the time.

Osborne didn't just want to build a truly affordable transportable computer, though; he also wanted to bundle serious business applications. So he used his stock to secure excellent deals on CP/M, WordStar and Microsoft MBASIC, and even had software chief Richard Frank create SuperCalc when VisiCalc's owners didn't play ball.

Osborne 1

Manufacturer: Osborne Computer Corporation
Model: Osborne 1

Launched: April 1981
Country of Origin: USA

COMPANY HISTORY

The Osborne Computer Corporation was incorporated in January 1981 by Adam Osborne, but it wasn't the first business to bear his name. Osborne was born in Thailand, in 1939, to British parents, and spent a large part of his early childhood in India. Osborne moved to the UK at age 11 and later graduated with a degree in chemical engineering from the University of Birmingham.
He then relocated to the US, where he completed his PhD before taking a job with Shell in California. A keen computer enthusiast, Osborne took up programming and writing technical books in his spare time, including a manual for Intel's 4004, which in 1971 was the world's first microprocessor. One year later, Osborne began writing manuals full-time, often selling them from a stall in computer clubs.
Osborne's title *An Introduction to Microcomputers* so impressed IMSAI's Bruce Van Natta that he bundled it with every machine sold. Osborne subsequently set up his own publishing company and later became an influential columnist for *Interface Age* (later *InfoWorld*) magazine.

SPECIFICATION
CPU model: Z80
Speed: 4MHz
RAM: 64KB
Special features: Transportable unit with built-in 5in monitor
Local price at launch: $1795

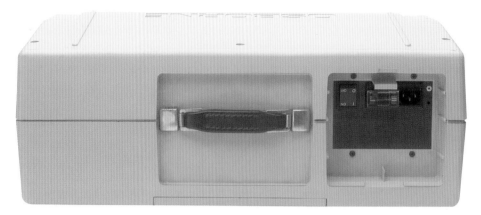

INPUT/OUTPUT

1 RS232
2 IEEE 488
3 Modem port
4 Composite video

Osborne 1

076_77

Manufacturer: Osborne Computer Corporation
Model: Osborne 1

WHAT HAPPENED NEXT

The Osborne 1 was launched in April 1981 and sold for $1795, but it also came with software worth that amount. Osborne reckoned he might sell 10,000 units over its lifespan, but he soon shifted this number every month. After all, buyers were effectively getting a free portable computer with every software bundle. Whether through a press leak or simple naïveté, news of the much-improved Osborne Executive model got out long before it actually became available. Anticipating the new model, dealers stopped buying the old one, and the resulting unsold stock contributed to Osborne Computer Corporation's financial failure. The company filed for bankruptcy in September 1983.

DID YOU KNOW?

Lee Felsenstein was an expert in digital displays and devised a cunning workaround for the Osborne 1's five-inch screen. The processor's 4MHz clock speed made the optimum character time one microsecond, which translated into fifty-two visible characters per line. In order to handle the 128-character width of standard displays, though, Felsenstein stored characters in memory and used keys to scroll around.

The Osborne 1 also featured a connector for a future modem, but its signals were left hanging on the final model. One such signal was an all-purpose control bit that Felsenstein labelled OLB for One Lousy Bit. Later, when writing the manual and needing official-sounding acronyms, Thom Hogan renamed it the Output Low Bit.

The Osborne's case design went through a revision early in the machine's life. The earlier Osborne 1 had a more rounded, beige form and a centre-mounted hinge for the keyboard. The 1A case (pictured) also became the "Executive" case.

During the late Seventies, IBM realized the new breed of personal computers could be a threat to its mainframe business and knew it had to develop its own affordable machine. IBM had, in fact, worked on the idea of personal computers for some time, but it hadn't succeeded in separating them from its traditional business. Its solution this time was to create an independent division in Boca Raton, Florida, that would have the freedom to buy components from any other company.

In September 1980, a core team of IBM researchers was dispatched to Boca Raton and given one year to develop a new personal computer. The key engineers were Rob Baker, Bill Tutt, Tom Anzelone, Jimmy Harris, Fred Goetz, Dick Clarke, Andy Saenz, Noel Fallwell, Dave Bradley, Patty McHugh, Bill Sydnes and Lewis Eggebrecht; Bradley is credited as the man behind CTRL-ALT-DEL.

As project "Chess" began in great secrecy, IBM received a cold call from Intel salesman Earl Whetstone wondering if it would be interested in a processor demonstration. Consequently, the IBM PC team ended up using the Intel 8088. It also bought an operating system from Microsoft.

Since any other company could simply buy the same off-the-shelf components and produce a direct clone, IBM sensibly copyrighted its BIOS system control code for the new computer.

IBM 5150 Personal Computer

Manufacturer: IBM
Name: PC 5150

Launched: August 1981
Country of Origin: USA

COMPANY HISTORY

IBM was formed in 1924, but it can be traced back as far as 1890, when German immigrant and statistician Herman Hollerith won a contest held by the US Census Bureau to find a more efficient way of handling its data. Hollerith's punched-card solution inspired him to form his own Tabulating Machine Company in 1896.

In 1911, trust organizer Charles Flint merged Hollerith's company with International Time Recording and the Computing Scale Company of America to form the Computing-Tabulating-Recording Company, or CTR for short. With products as diverse as punch cards to cheese slicers, though, Flint had a management nightmare on his hands. He hired Tom Watson – who had been second in command at the National Cash Register company – as general manager.

Watson instilled pride and loyalty into every worker at CTR, pioneering sales incentives, group life-insurance, paid holidays, team outings, employee sports teams and even a company band. In less than a year, he became president of CTR, and, in 1924, he changed the company name to International Business Machines Corporation, or IBM.

SPECIFICATION

CPU model: Intel 8088
Speed: 4.77MHz
RAM: 16KB
Special features: BASIC in ROM
Local price at launch: $1565

IBM 5150 Personal Computer

080_81

Manufacturer: IBM
Name: PC 5150

WHAT HAPPENED NEXT

IBM announced its 5150 Personal Computer in New York on 13th August 1981, which soon began to sell much better than expected, a result that proved particularly fortuitous for Intel and Microsoft. Before long, the term PC would refer almost exclusively to an IBM model, despite it being equally applicable to machines from the likes of Apple and Commodore. IBM followed it up with the PC XT in 1983 and the PC AT in 1984, but a more important event occurred earlier in November 1982. A new company called Compaq figured a way to reverse-engineer IBM's BIOS and produce a legal clone, forever changing the IT industry and securing the fortunes of Intel and Microsoft.

The IBM PC's success certainly was not in breaking any technical frontiers. It was significantly less powerful than many 8-bit machines of the day, but what it did have was the styling and branding of IBM. Many companies simply didn't consider a PC worth having until IBM offered one.

INPUT/OUTPUT
1 5x 8-bit ISA slots
2 Monitor
3 Centronics
4 Cassette

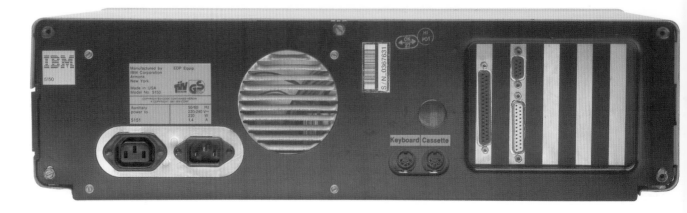

DID YOU KNOW?

The story behind how **IBM** and **Microsoft** got together is a favourite of IT folklore, though we may never truly know the facts. What follows is the most likely story. **IBM**'s personal computer team arranged several secretive meetings with Microsoft during 1980 to discuss software, including the company's BASIC programming language, for its project. IBM also needed an operating system, but not yet being in this business, Bill Gates put the PC team onto Gary Kildall, creator of the well-known CP/M.

Legend has it Kildall was out when IBM paid a visit to his Digital Research HQ, and the person they met was understandably wary of signing secretive nondisclosure agreements. IBM returned to Microsoft and Gates didn't need to think twice; the trouble was, he didn't have an operating system to offer. Tim Patterson of neighbouring Seattle Computer Products had developed his own OS for the Intel 8086. Gates bought it and hired Patterson to adapt it for the IBM's 8088 processor, then launched it with the PC as **MS-DOS version 1.0**. This was adapted and rebranded as **PC-DOS** for IBM.

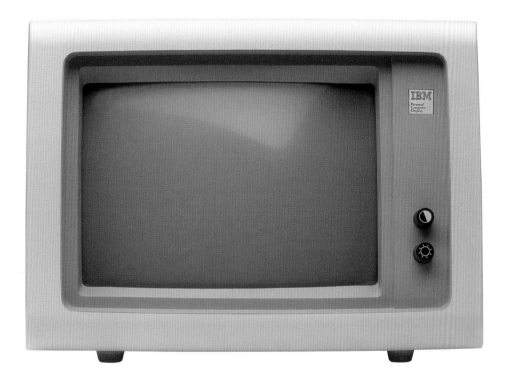

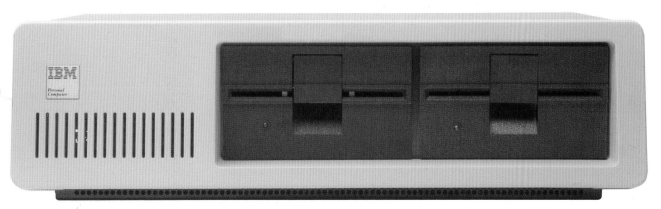

BBC Micro Model A/B

During early 1981, the BBC's Computer Literacy Project hit a problem. The NewBrain computer *(p102),* which had originally been earmarked to become the BBC Micro, hit production difficulties. Over at Acorn, work had begun on the Proton, and when cofounder Chris Curry heard the BBC was looking for a new computer, he persuaded them to come for a demonstration. The only problem was that the BBC was arriving the following Friday, and the Proton didn't yet physically exist.

Acorn's other cofounder, Hermann Hauser, had a plan. On Sunday evening, he made separate calls to Sophie Wilson, designer of Acorn's original System-1, and Steve Furber, a longtime Acorn collaborator, to ask if they could build a working prototype in five days. Both thought it would be impossible, but Hauser convinced each that the other had said it could be done, and they agreed to give it a try.

Over the next two days, Wilson and Furber turned their plans into a working circuit diagram and managed to source brand-new memory chips from a Hitachi salesman on Wednesday. On Thursday, Wilson, Furber and Hauser, along with Acorn chief engineer Chris Turner and Ramanuj "Ram" Banerjee from the Cambridge University Computer Lab, started building the prototype. The machine finally came to life at seven the following morning, leaving Wilson just three hours to port enough of an operating system to get it started.

Manufacturer: Acorn Computers Ltd	**Launched:** December 1981
Name: BBC Micro	**Country of Origin:** England

SPECIFICATION

CPU model: 6502
Speed: 2MHz
RAM: 16KB (Model A), 32KB (Model B)
Special features: Multiple graphics modes including Teletext and 640 x 256
Local price at launch: £235 (Model A), £335 (Model B)

COMPANY HISTORY

See Acorn Atom, p62

BACKGROUND

In 1979, British psychologist and computer scientist Dr. Christopher Riche Evans wrote a book called *The Mighty Micro: The Impact of the Computer Revolution*, which the BBC later adapted into a series. This series proved sufficiently influential for the BBC to launch the Computer Literacy Project, aimed at increasing the British public's understanding of computers with the help of a new TV series, a BBC-branded computer and the backing of the British government.

BBC Micro
Model A/B

084_85

Manufacturer: Acorn Computers Ltd
Name: BBC Micro

INPUT/OUTPUT

1 UHF TV out
2 BNC video out
3 RGB video out
4 RS423
5 Cassette
6 Analogue In (DB15)
7 Econet (Acorn network)
8 TUBE interface
9 1MHz bus
10 User port
11 Printer port
12 Disk-drive connector

WHAT HAPPENED NEXT
The visiting BBC engineers were sufficiently impressed by the Proton demonstration to award Acorn the contract in April 1981. The BBC Micro specification was subsequently finalized with no fewer than eight graphics modes, including Teletext. Two versions were officially launched that November: the 16KB Model A at £235 and the 32KB Model B at £335. Despite its higher price and a later increase to £399, the Model B far outsold the Model A. Acorn then developed the Electron to fill the gap for a budget home computer.
Later BBC Micros included the Model B+, with 64KB RAM, and the BBC Master. Acorn was originally contracted to build 12,000 units, but the BBC Micro ended up selling over two million worldwide.

Designed by **Acorn Computers Limited, Cambridge. England** ©1981 Registered design.

UHF out   video out   RGB   RS423   cassette   analogue in   econet

Manufactured to BS415
by BSR (UK)

On   220-240V~
     50/60 HZ
     50 - WATTS

Off

DID YOU KNOW?

The BBC Micro was incredibly successful in the educational market, ending up being the preferred computer in seven out of ten UK schools. This, in turn, made it come across as less fun than its cheaper rivals, but this bias was completely reversed by a single software title. Ian Bell and David Braben's groundbreaking *Elite* delivered a vast universe in 3D wireframe graphics, which proved so compelling that many children begged their parents to buy a BBC Micro just to play the game.

The TUBE bus, to the left of the underside of the computer, allowed the connection of other processors to the BBC Micro. These included the 6502, Z80, 68000 and the ARM 1, a RISC chip whose future was in Acorn's groundbreaking Archimedes machines *(see p178)*.

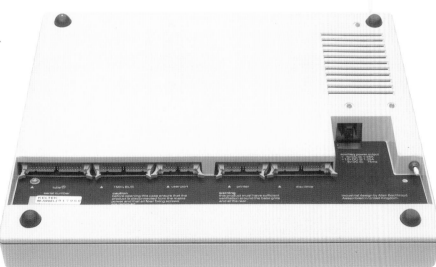

Commodore 64

As the VIC-20 launched in early 1981, Commodore's semiconductor engineers were working on video and audio chips for what would be a state-of-the-art arcade machine. This project was headed by Albert Charpentier, who'd managed the electronics behind the VIC-20. Charpentier developed the graphics component, and VIC veteran Bob Yannes, a music hobbyist, was assigned the audio chip.

By the time the Video Interface Chip II (VIC-II 6567) and Sound Interface Device (SID 6581) chip were completed, though, the arcade market had collapsed. Since the VIC-20 was selling like hotcakes, it was clear that the best use of these new chips would be in a follow-up. So in autumn 1981, work began on a 64KB home computer employing the VIC-II and SID with the VIC-20's case and keyboard. Its 6510 main processor was based on the standard 6502, but modified to address more memory.

By December 1981, the components were operational, allowing four units to be assembled for the January 1982 Consumer Electronics Show. Crucially, by exploiting parts originally designed for an adaptable arcade machine, Commodore's new system boasted far greater graphics and audio capabilities than any home computer of the time. Charpentier's VIC-II allowed 8 hardware sprites, while Yannes's SID chip was a highly impressive three-voice synthesizer with independent oscillators.

Manufacturer: Commodore	**Launched:** January 1982
Model: CBM-64	**Country of Origin:** USA

SPECIFICATION

CPU model: 6510
Speed: 1MHz
RAM: 64KB
Special features: VIC-II graphics and SID synthesiser chips
Local price at launch: $599

COMPANY HISTORY

See **Commodore PET 2001, p16**

Commodore 64

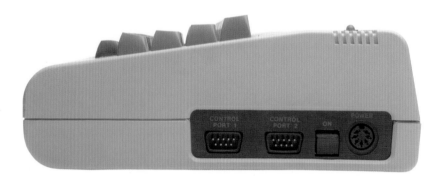

Manufacturer: Commodore
Model: CBM-64

INPUT/OUTPUT

1 RGB (composite,
  chroma/luma and sound)
2 2x joystick
3 Cartridge slot
4 Tape interface (300 bps)
5 Serial port
6 User port
7 TV RF output

WHAT HAPPENED NEXT

The Commodore 64 may have initially cost twice as much as the VIC-20 but, with all its features, it became wildly popular. Estimates widely vary, but at least 16 million CBM-64s are thought to have been sold, making it the best-selling home computer ever. Several follow-ups were launched, including the Commodore 128 and the luggable SX64 with built-in colour monitor and disk drive. Later C64s came in slimmer white cases; and, to celebrate its millionth sale in Germany, two-hundred golden and extremely rare CBM-64s were produced. Aggressive price drops to force TI out of the market, however, made Tramiel unpopular with the Commodore board. He left in January 1984, later buying Atari and launching the ST range.

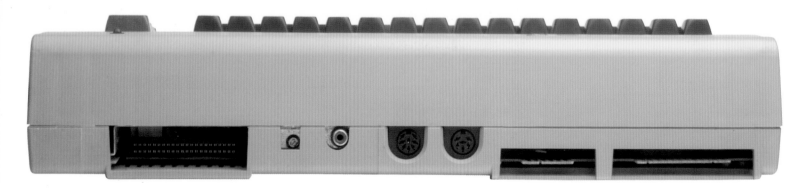

64K was a lot of memory in the C64's day, and Commodore chose to make a lot of its comparative price point in their advertising campaign, comparing the machine's sub-$600 price tag to the Apple IIe and the IBM PC's, both coming in at around $1350 at the time.

DID YOU KNOW?

After developing the chipsets behind both the VIC-20 and CBM-64, Al Charpentier and Bob Yannes, along with fellow Commodore engineer Bruce Crockett, left in 1982 to form synthesizer company Ensoniq. They developed a chip for a low-cost sampler called the Mirage and used it to produce a software drum-machine. Ensoniq later became a big name in synthesizers and was acquired by Creative Labs in 1997. Such was the influence of Bob Yannes's original SID chip that many Web forums still fondly discuss Commodore 64 game music composed by the likes of Rob Hubbard and Martin Galway.

Sinclair ZX Spectrum

For the ZX81's successor, Clive Sinclair had two main goals: to address criticisms of its flat keyboard, while introducing colour capabilities.

Rick Dickinson, designer of the ZX81 case, was given the task of devising something more tactile while still on a tight budget. Davis Southward of Sinclair's portable TV team came up with the idea of using rubber keys, which Dickinson subsequently developed into a single sheet with a thin metal overlay.

Richard Altwasser, who joined Sinclair mid-way through ZX81 development, was appointed project leader for the new hardware, which had to be Z80-based to re-use code from the earlier models. Altwasser designed the circuits and a new custom ULA chip by hand on a drafting box, with the aid of a calculator for timings. The new machine would have colour, but to minimize memory could only apply it to entire character blocks and not individual pixels.

The ROM size doubled again to 16KB and as with previous ZX models, the code was out-sourced to Nine Tiles, with Steve Vickers writing the lion's share; again, code was recycled, with the ZX80's original 4KB present.

Sinclair wanted a name to reflect its colour capabilities, but Spectrum was actually coined by division head Nigel Searle's girlfriend. It was launched in April 1982 with either 16 or 48KB of RAM.

Manufacturer: Sinclair
Model: ZX Spectrum

Launched: April 1982
Country of Origin: England

SPECIFICATION
CPU model: Z80A
Speed: 3.5MHz
RAM: 16KB or 48KB
Special features: Rubber keyboard, color and sound capabilities
Local price at launch: £125 (16KB version), £175 (48KB version)

COMPANY HISTORY
See Sinclair ZX80, p58.

Sinclair ZX Spectrum

Manufacturer: Sinclair
Model: ZXSpectrum

WHAT HAPPENED NEXT

The ZX Spectrum was an enormous success, becoming Britain's best-selling micro and spawning a huge market for software and peripherals. Along with Sinclair's own MicroDrives, which stored 85KB of data on tiny tape cartridges, third-party successes included the ubiquitous Kempston joystick interface. In 1984, Sinclair launched the Spectrum+, which featured a new case and keyboard, while Timex produced the TS-2048 and TS-2068 versions for the US market. Sinclair later produced the Spectrum 128 and QL but ran into financial troubles, eventually selling rights to produce the ZX range to Amstrad in 1986. Amstrad later released three enhanced versions: Spectrum +2, Spectrum +3 and finally the Spectrum +2A in 1988.

INPUT/OUTPUT

1 Expansion port
2 Tape recorder (1200 baud)
3 RF video out

The ZX Spectrum's single expansion port became the gateway to a huge range of add-ons, each sporting Sinclair's distinctive styling. The most famous of these was the MicroDrive, which read and wrote to tiny 85KB cassettes of 2mm wide magnetic tape. With an average access time of 3.5 seconds, these appeared an elegant solution in comparison to a tape recorder; however they were let down by reliability problems.

DID YOU KNOW?

The Spectrum may have offered a lot of computer for the money, but its enormous success can mostly be attributed to a wealth of quality games. Perhaps more surprising though was just how good many of them were, considering the Spectrum's hardware limitations.

During the Spectrum's golden years, many games programmers and publishers gained legendary status. Some programmers became household names, such as Mathew Smith (of *Manic Miner* and *Jet Set Willy*) and Imagine's Eugene Evans, who famously bought himself an expensive sports car before being able to drive.

Other software houses included Ocean, Melbourne House and probably most legendary of all, Ultimate *Play The Game*. Ultimate's games managed to push the Spectrum further than anyone believed possible, from the sheer speed of their debut *Jet Pac*, to the 3D isometric adventure *Knight Lore*, which amazingly was finished before its two prequels. Fans of Ultimate can rest assure they're still producing games today under the Rare brand which, after creating several Nintendo classics including *Goldeneye*, was recently bought by Microsoft Game Studios. The old Ultimate humour can still be seen in the X-Box title, *Grabbed by the Ghoulies*.

Coleco enjoyed brief success with small table-top clones of arcade machines in the early Eighties, but it became clear a programmable games console was required to compete in the lucrative market owned by the Atari VCS and, to a lesser extent, Mattel's IntelliVision.

Indeed legend has it Atari and Mattel were so focused on being fierce rivals, neither was aware Coleco had been quietly developing a technically superior competitor. Along with a Z80A processor and 8KB RAM, the Coleco console featured advanced sound and graphics chips from Texas Instruments, allowing it to come close to, or even match, many existing arcade coin-ops.

The elongated case design, doubling as storage for its pair of rectangular controllers, was borrowed straight from Mattel's IntelliVision, but stubby joysticks were employed rather than Mattel's disc pads.

Coleco knew it had to launch its console with a high-profile arcade licence, and beat both Atari and Mattel to license Nintendo's *Donkey Kong*. Unbeknown to Coleco though was Universal Studio's impending legal action against Nintendo (and now Coleco) over infringement of the King Kong copyright. Although Nintendo fought and won, Coleco allegedly settled out of court for 3% of game royalties; it launched the ColecoVision console with *Donkey Kong* in June 1982.

Coleco Vision

Manufacturer: Coleco
Model: Vision

Launched: June 1982
Country of Origin: USA

COMPANY HISTORY

The Connecticut Leather Company was formed by Russian immigrant Maurice Greenburg in 1932. Trading out of West Hartford, Connecticut, the company initially distributed leather products to shoe-makers. During the early Fifties, Greenburg's son Leonard built a leather-cutting machine and started selling craft kits; around this time, the company name was shortened to Coleco.

During the late Fifties, Coleco moved into plastic products, including a highly successful line of wading pools. Understandably concerned about relying on such a seasonal product, Leonard and his brother Arnold started looking into alternatives to supplement the pool business. Some proved more successful than others, but one took the company in an entirely new direction: video games. In 1972, Atari had released its *Pong* arcade machine and Coleco decided to produce a home version. Atari beat Coleco to market with its own home version of *Pong* in 1975, but Coleco undercut it with its Telstar console the following year. Atari's later programmable VCS console however killed the Telstar, forcing Coleco to rethink.

SPECIFICATION

CPU model: Z80A
Speed: 3.57MHz
RAM: 8KB
Special features: TI graphics and audio processors, controllers with numeric keypads
Local price at launch: $195

1982

Coleco
Vision

096_97

Manufacturer: Coleco
Model: Vision

The Coleco's controllers went through a number of revisions during the machine's development. Finger rollers were to have been added between the keypad and joystick, a secret the circuit board will reveal. Side buttons were eventually introduced on the later "Super Action Controller".

WHAT HAPPENED NEXT

Within six months of release, the ColecoVision shot to number one position, and continued to impress with near-perfect conversions of other, albeit often obscure, arcade games. Particularly impressive were the 3D isometric scrolling of *Zaxxon* and the cartoon-like animation of *Smurf*.

The ColecoVision also offered three expansion modules, the first allowing it to play Atari VCS games, while the second was a proper steering wheel and pedals sold with the *Turbo* driving game.

The third was the particularly ambitious *Adam*, which transformed the ColecoVision into a home computer featuring a keyboard, a pair of 256KB cassette drives and a daisy wheel printer. Sadly, by the time *Adam* arrived, the home computer market had crashed, forcing Coleco to halt production in 1984.

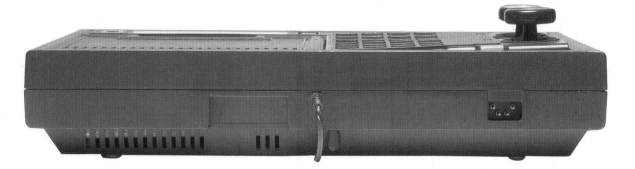

The overall console design owes a great deal to the Intellivision, with the controller housing slots. However the Coleco doesn't place the cartridge slot away to the side, but on the top like modern consoles. That leaves room at the front for the expansion slot.

DID YOU KNOW?

Along with the three famous expansion units, Coleco promised several more peripherals that never quite made it to market. Most impressive of all was the CED vinyl video record adapter, which would allow it to play a perfect version of former Disney artist Don Bluth's arcade classic *Dragon's Lair*.

Coleco briefly recovered from the video game crash by launching Cabbage Patch Dolls, but by 1988 filed for bankruptcy and sold its assets to Hasbro the following year.

1982

GCE / MB
Vectrex

098_99

The Vectrex began life in early 1981 after Western Technologies/Smith Engineering acquired a number of 5in cathode ray tubes from a liquidator's surplus store. Employees Mike Purvis and John Ross suggested they could be used as the display of an all-in-one games console, an idea which head of engineering Jay Smith approved.

The project started life as the Mini Arcade and was initially optioned by Kenner before The General Consumer Electronics company (GCE) licensed it that fall. GCE's boss Ed Krakauer liked the idea of the console, but changed the screen size to 9in. John Ross designed the hardware, with Gerry Karr and John Hall writing its ROM, which was called The Executive.

Hall later left to write the *Mine Storm* game, which was built into the console, leaving Karr to rewrite the ROM with the help of Duncan Muirhead who developed many of the trigonometric routines. After rejecting the name Vector-X in a brainstorming session, the final Vectrex name was coined.

The Vectrex was unique among its peers, not just for having a built-in screen, but one which employed oscilloscope vector technology. This could draw perfectly straight diagonal lines, unlike the jagged staircases of the common raster technology. Since the display was black and white though, Vectrex games were supplied with clip-on coloured acetate overlays.

Manufacturer: GCE / Milton Bradley	**Launched:** June 1982
Model: Vectrex	**Country of Origin:** USA

SPECIFICATION

CPU model: Motorola 6809
Speed: 1MHz
RAM: 3.5KB
Special features: 9in black and white vector monitor, control panel with four buttons and self-centring analogue joystick
Local price at launch: $199

COMPANY HISTORY

While the Vectrex was originally launched by GCE, the company most associated with it was games giant Milton Bradley, which acquired GCE in 1983. Milton Bradley the company was formed by the man of the same name in 1864. Bradley, born in Vienna, Maine, started his career in printing, opening Massachusetts's first colour lithography shop in 1860.

Soon after opening his shop, Bradley met with a friend who had a new board game believed to have been imported from Europe. It employed a spinner to determine how far a player could proceed, which inspired Bradley to devise his own board game.

In Bradley's *Checkered Game of Life*, players used a spinning dial to plot their course around a board, hoping to land on squares leading to happy retirement and not bankruptcy. By 1861, Bradley had sold over 45,000 copies and three years later formed his own company to sell these and other printed games.

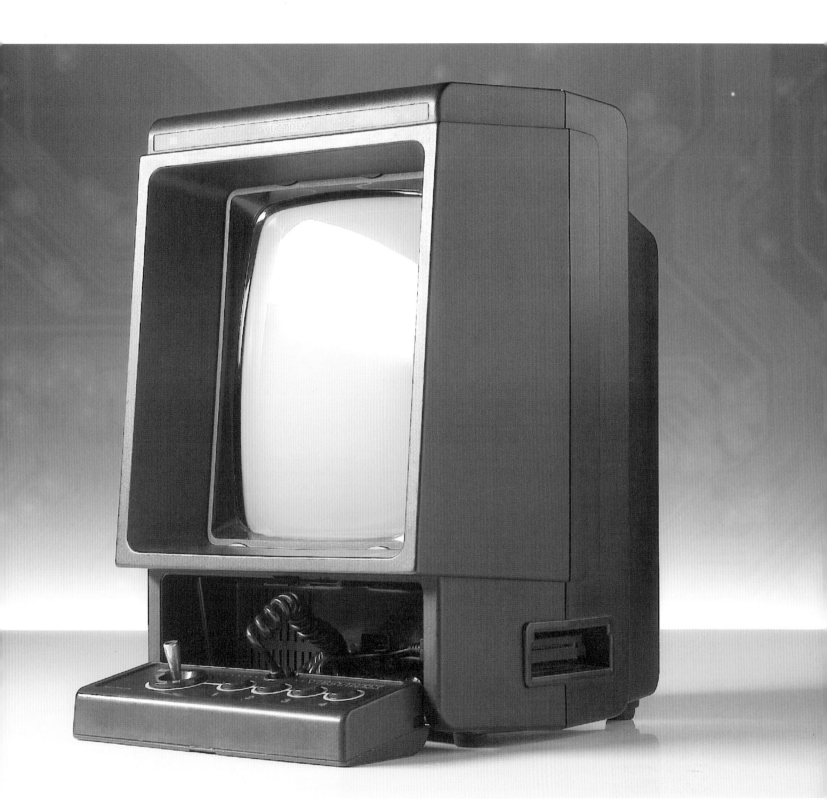

GCE / MB
Vectrex

Manufacturer: GCE / Milton Bradley
Model: Vectrex

WHAT HAPPENED NEXT

GCE launched the Vectrex at the June 1982 Consumer Electronics Show. With a built-in screen, loudspeaker and arcade-style controls, it was the closest thing to having a coin-op at home; indeed the supplied *Mine Storm* game was arguably the most accurate home version of Atari *Asteroids*, which itself employed a vector display. While the best Vectrex games like *Web Warp* were also inspired from vector-based arcade coin-ops, several raster-based titles were successfully converted – including *Scramble* and *Berzerk*.

In spring 1983, GCE was bought by Milton Bradley, which allowed the Vectrex to be sold throughout Europe. By early 1984, though, the video games market had crashed, forcing the end of Vectrex production. Hasbro bought Milton Bradley later that year.

The Vectrex took a very different approach to other systems at the time. By not including a second controller, which other consoles did, the Vectrex moved further away from the *Pong* heritage. Equally the inclusion of a screen prevented monopolizing the family TV space.

DID YOU KNOW?

As with other games consoles of the period, the Vectrex enjoyed several peripherals and rumours of many more. Along with a spare control panel for two-player games, a lightpen was released with a simple art package. 3D glasses, which also delivered basic colour, were also developed, but barely made it beyond demonstrations at trade shows. Colour graphics was something the Vectrex desperately wanted, and a number of colour prototype versions were developed, but none came to market. There was even a rumour of a home computer add-on unit. Legend has it Western Technologies/Smith Engineering began work on a handheld Vectrex in 1988, perhaps using Sinclair's pocket flat TV technology, but Nintendo's GameBoy handheld scuppered the plan.

Grundy NewBrain

Newbury Labs completed Radionics work and announced the NewBrain with a handful of working prototypes in 1980. The NewBrain certainly looked way ahead of its time: a portable computer about the size of a hardback book, with options for a built-in display and battery operation.

The cream case with brown keys and lettering may have matched Newbury Labs' colours, but this was more fortuitous coincidence than actual design. The prototype NewBrains only sported these colours because that's what the case manufacturer had available at the time. The final models were to be red and grey, but since this would involve retooling at additional cost, the prototype cream and brown cases made it to the stores.

Newbury then went through a process of streamlining, with its MD leaving to join the Grundy Group and the NewBrain following shortly afterwards. Grundy Business Systems (GBS) was set up in late 1981 to market and produce the NewBrain, which eventually made it to the shops in the summer of 1982.

The NewBrain Model A cost £233 and featured a 4MHz Z80A processor, display resolutions up to 640 x 250 pixels, and 32KB of RAM expandable to a massive 2MB. The £267 AD model additionally boasted a 16-character green fluorescent display and the ability to run from an optional battery.

Manufacturer: Grundy Business Systems
Name: NewBrain

Launched: July 1982
Country of Origin: England

SPECIFICATION

CPU model: Z80A
Speed: 4MHz
RAM: 32KB
Special features: AD model featured built-in 16 character display and optional battery
Local price at launch: £233 (Model A), £267 (Model AD)

COMPANY HISTORY

The NewBrain computer was connected to three different companies before finally being launched. The project began at Clive Sinclair's Radionics company, originally founded on 25th July 1961. Sinclair had previously launched the MK14 computer kit in 1977 and was keen to follow it up with a highly affordable system for the man on the street.

Work began on the new Radionics computer during the summer of 1978, funded by the UK Government's National Enterprise Board, NEB. Mike Wakefield was the designer and Basil Smith worked on software, but before it could be completed, NEB ran into troubles and announced plans to sell off Radionics' calculator and TV interests.

NEB thought the Radionics computer too promising to abandon, so transferred it to another government-funded company, VDU manufacturer Newbury Labs. Radionics was subsequently closed in mid-1979, with Sinclair taking a golden handshake and starting work on the ZX80 under his Science of Cambridge brand.

Grundy NewBrain

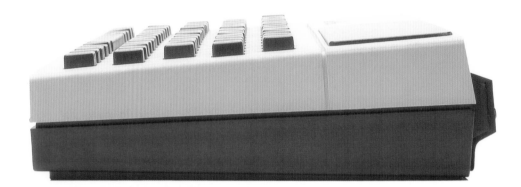

Manufacturer: Grundy Business Systems
Name: NewBrain

INPUT/OUTPUT

1 2x tape (1200 baud)
2 RGB
3 UHF
4 2x RS232c (the one marked "printer" lacked an in line)
5 Z80 bus

WHAT HAPPENED NEXT

The NewBrain boasted an impressive array of expansion options including the ability to run CPM, but few were available at launch and there was little quality software, too. Worse, while impressive when announced in 1980, the NewBrain had simply lost its chance by the time it finally went on sale. Over-production of NewBrains in 1983 as the market began to collapse forced the Grundy Group to pull the plug on GBS later that year. Some time afterwards the remaining NewBrain stock was bought by Dutch company Tradecom, which had a government contract to supply schools in Holland with computers. Subsequent developments from Norwegian and Danish companies saw the NewBrain enjoy its final days equipped with the peripherals it deserved.

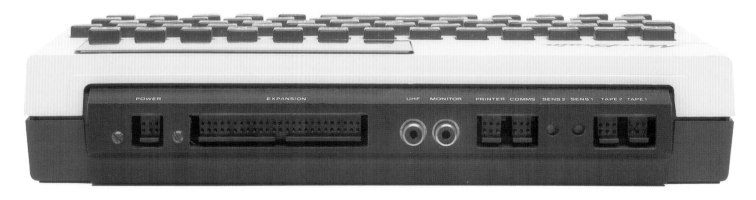

POWER　　　　EXPANSION　　　　UHF　MONITOR　　PRINTER　COMMS　SENS 2　SENS 1　TAPE 2　TAPE 1

The NewBrain's second tape socket made it possible to read data in one, perform calculations and output the results to another. One machine found a home at the Angolan Ministry of Commerce, doing the job of an IBM 370 mainframe, the cassettes acting a little like punched cards.

DID YOU KNOW?

Legend has it the NewBrain was originally ear-marked to become the BBC Micro. The BBC was on the lookout for a British home computer to brand for its new TV series and campaign, and the early NewBrain specification appeared to fit the bill. The story goes that production difficulties at Newbury Labs forced the BBC to look elsewhere.

What's known for sure is Chris Curry from Acorn got wind the BBC was looking for a computer to brand and persuaded them to consider the Proton. Acorn won the contract and the Proton was developed into the BBC Micro.

Dragon 32

During the early Eighties, Mettoy managing director Tony Clarke realized children were becoming more interested in home computers than in the traditional toys his company produced. To tap into this new market, Clarke initiated project SAM to build a home computer under Mettoy's existing Dragon Data brand.

The hardware design was undertaken externally and ended up bearing a strong resemblance to the Tandy TRS-80 Colour Computer. The design team was in contact with Motorola's semiconductor base in Scotland and employed the same Motorola 6809 processor, video and interfacing chips as the Tandy. Project SAM even featured the same keyboard layout, cartridge connector, joystick ports and memory map; and both SAM and Tandy went to Microsoft for a BASIC interpreter.

To avoid legal conflict, Dragon Data fitted its machine with a proper parallel printer port and sufficient memory to run Microsoft's Extended BASIC; the first Tandys only featured 4 or 8KB RAM. Interestingly, Dragon Data originally intended to use only 16KB of memory but upgraded to 32KB to compete with Sinclair's upgraded Spectrum. Dragon Data also modified the BIOS to briefly display its programmer's initials: DNS, for Duncan Smeed. Lyndon Davies hand-soldered the first batch of prototypes, and the final production models were ready in August 1982.

Manufacturer: Dragon Data
Name: Dragon 32

Launched: August 1982
Country of Origin: Wales

SPECIFICATION

CPU model: Motorola 6809
Speed: 1MHz
RAM: 32KB
Special features: Uncanny resemblance to Tandy TRS-80 Colour Computer
Local price at launch: £199

COMPANY HISTORY

Dragon Data was formed in the mid-Seventies as a division of English toy manufacturer Mettoy, founded by Philip Ullman in 1933. Ullman, once the proprietor of German tin-plate toy company Tipp & Co., had escaped the rise of the Nazis by setting up a new company in the UK using money owed to him by British department store Marks & Spencer. He subsequently founded Mettoy in Northampton, naming it after "metal toys". After the war, Mettoy relocated to

Swansea, in Wales, where it distributed Canadian Aurora plastic-model kits along with marketing the Playtown range of railway construction kits. Mettoy later abandoned tin-plate toys in favour of die-cast models, which included the legendary Corgi brand. As Mettoy evolved, it became sufficiently large to justify setting up its own computer bureau division to process data for smaller companies. Based in Wales, it was named Dragon Data, after that country's national emblem.

Dragon 32

Manufacturer: Dragon Data
Name: Dragon 32

INPUT/OUTPUT
1 RF TV out
2 2x analogne joystick
3 Cassette
4 Centronics parallel port
5 Cartridge slot
6 Composite monitor

WHAT HAPPENED NEXT
While retailers W H Smith and John Menzies had their hands full with Sinclair and Commodore computers, Dragon Data secured deals with Boots, Comet and Dixons to sell its new machine. By 1983, no fewer than 40,000 units had been sold. With investment from Prudential and the Welsh Development Agency, Dragon Data expanded and launched the Dragon 64 in the UK and US in autumn 1983. As the market began to slump that winter,

though, GEC took over management. In May 1984, GEC Dragon announced a portable 64KB model and spoke of two new systems, including a drive-packed Dragon 64 and dual-6809 machine. One month later, though, Dragon announced bankruptcy. Spanish company Eurohard SA bought Dragon Data, supplying around 20,000 Dragons to Spanish schools. Most were actually given away, with Eurohard gradually closing its factories over the subsequent years.

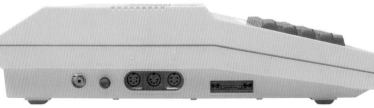

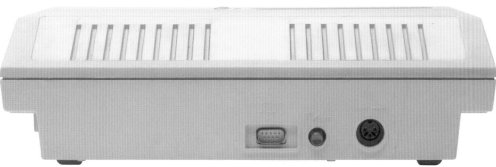

Dragon's domestic marketing campaign centred not only on the machine's UK heritage but also on its robustness, boasting of the high-quality, typewriter-style keyboard – "guaranteed for twenty million depressions" – and a case strong enough to support a television set or monitor.

DID YOU KNOW?
A little-known fact about Dragon Data was that it produced a software package for the UK agriculture community that allowed farmers to keep track of cows and other livestock. This Farm Fax package was sold with the Dragon 32 as part of a government scheme to encourage farmers to use computers.

Jupiter ACE

The Jupiter ACE was designed by Richard Altwasser and Steve Vickers, who were previously responsible for much of the Sinclair ZX Spectrum.

Unsurprisingly, given their previous work with Sinclair, Vickers and Altwasser adopted that company's successful strategy of designing a computer to meet a strict price point. The Jupiter ACE was a highly compact system with a chicklet-style keyboard and a startling resemblance to the Sinclair ZX81, only finished in white with red stripes.

The ACE's insides were also closer to the ZX81's than to the Spectrum's, with the same 3.5MHz Z80A processor and just 3KB of RAM. Unlike the ZX81, though, the ACE did feature sound capabilities. Oddly, after making colour a standard in the Spectrum, Altwasser and Vickers equipped the ACE with black-and-white graphics.

At the time, as virtually every machine came with BASIC, Vickers and Altwasser felt it would be difficult to compete. So they chose the FORTH programming language as a unique selling point. FORTH had the benefit of being both compact and fast – which fit the ACE's specifications perfectly – and it was also enjoying a high profile after a special edition of *BYTE* magazine.

The use of FORTH and a modest hardware specification allowed the Jupiter ACE to be both fast and inexpensive, retailing for just £89.99.

Manufacturer: Jupiter Cantab
Name: ACE

Launched: September 1982
Country of Origin: England

SPECIFICATION

CPU model: Z80A
Speed: 3.5MHz
RAM: 3KB
Special features: First home computer to employ FORTH programming language
Local price at launch: £89.99

COMPANY HISTORY

Jupiter Cantab was formed by Steve Vickers and Richard Altwasser in 1982. Vickers had worked for John Grant's Nine Tiles company, which wrote the code for Sinclair's computers, while Altwasser had worked for Sinclair Research itself. The pair are credited for much of the Spectrum, Vickers writing its ROM and Altwasser designing its hardware.

After completing the Spectrum, Altwasser and Vickers decided to start their own company. Both had enjoyed working on Sinclair's tough deadlines but now wanted to be their own bosses. They initially traded under the name Rainbow, the name Altwasser had originally suggested Sinclair should call the machine that became the ZX Spectrum. Upon discovering that Rainbow was already in use, they chose Jupiter Cantab instead. Cantab is short for Cantabridgian (meaning "of Cambridge"). It seemed appropriate: Both Vickers and Altwasser held University of Cambridge degrees and had worked with Sinclair there.

Jupiter ACE

Manufacturer: Jupiter Cantab
Name: ACE

WHAT HAPPENED NEXT

The Jupiter ACE sold well to people who were happy to play with FORTH, but sadly, it never grew beyond that market because it never built up a large body of software. By 1984, Jupiter Cantab had gone bust, the liquidators selling its remaining stocks and FORTH rights to Boldfield Computing.

Boldfield then commissioned software, including games and a database, and introduced accessories like memory packs, monitor adapters and a full-size keyboard. These and the ACE were sold via mail order, but Boldfield never built any more units, instead running the project down after a couple of years as stocks dried up.

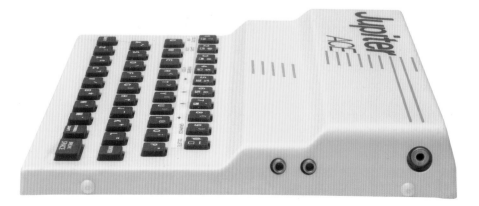

INPUT/OUTPUT
1 UHF TV out
2 User port
3 Tape (1500 baud)
4 Z80 bus

digital : retro

The ACE's marketing was targeted firmly at the hobbyist-programmer market created by computers like the Sinclair ZX80. Whereas other ads highlighted family credentials like joystick ports and educational software, the ACE's campaign focused on the speed of processing certain instructions. One thousand empty-look instructions would take, for example, 0.12 seconds on the ACE, compared to 0.67 seconds on the BBC Micro and 17.7 seconds on the Spectrum ZX81.

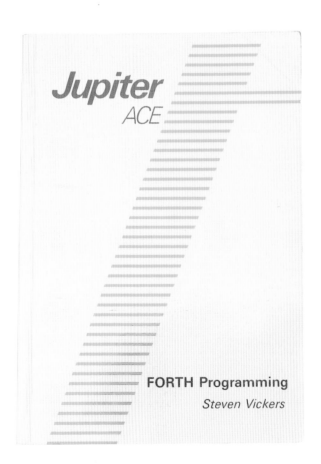

PRINTER BOARD

DID YOU KNOW?
In 1986, Richard Altwasser joined Amstrad, which had since bought the rights to produce Sinclair's ZX range. On his first day, Altwasser was called into the office of Bob Watkins (now Amstrad's group development and manufacturing director) to look over some circuit diagrams. Altwasser recalls, "I don't know whether Bob or I was more surprised to see that they were of the Spectrum, drawn and signed by me several years earlier."

The FORTH programming language runs programs three to ten times faster than BASIC, but it is procedure-based and harder to learn.

Compaq was formed with the sole intention of producing a portable IBM PC clone, but it had one big legal hurdle to overcome.

IBM may have used off-the-shelf components to build its Personal Computer and famously approached Microsoft to provide the OS, but Big Blue had sensibly copyrighted its BIOS. It may just have been a simple piece of code used by the computer as it powered up, but without it, you couldn't produce a compatible system.

Rather than illegally copy IBM's BIOS, Compaq's solution was to independently produce its own version from scratch that happened to be 100 percent compatible. The process it used to achieve this is known as reverse-engineering in a clean environment, where you can legally demonstrate no direct copying has taken place.

Compaq employed two teams of engineers who had no direct contact with each other. The first had access to IBM's BIOS code and made precise notes of what it did under every circumstance. Once passed by lawyers to ensure there was no violation of copyright, this specification was used by the second team to produce its own BIOS code from scratch. Since the second team could be proved not to have had contact with IBM's code, the process didn't violate the copyright. The project cost Compaq a reported $1 million, but it could now produce an IBM clone.

Compaq Portable Computer

Manufacturer: Compaq
Name: Portable Computer Mark I
(Mark III pictured)

Launched: November 1982
Country of Origin: USA

COMPANY HISTORY

Compaq was formed in February 1982 by Rod Canion, Jim Harris and Bill Murto. All three were senior managers at Texas Instruments who'd become restless. They'd witnessed IBM launch its Personal Computer in August 1981 and realized it was the future of business computing. Each invested $1,000 of his own money to found a company that would produce not only the first IBM PC clone, but make it portable, too. They sketched their concept on a paper place-mat in a Houston, Texas, pie shop.

Requiring significant investment, the idea was presented to former high-tech journalist Ben Rosen, who'd become president of venture capital firm Sevin-Rosen Partners. Rosen liked what he saw, provided funding and became company chairman, Canion taking the chief executive role.

SPECIFICATION

CPU model: Intel 8088
Speed: 4.77MHz
RAM: 128KB
Special features: Mark I: 9in monitor, pair of 5.25in floppy drives, portable design, the first legal IBM PC clone
Local price at launch: $2999

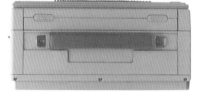

1982

Compaq Portable Computer

116_117

Manufacturer: Compaq
Name: Portable Computer Mark I
(Mark III pictured)

WHAT HAPPENED NEXT

Compaq's debut machine was the first legal IBM clone. It was portable, too, with a nine-inch monitor and weight of "just" thirty-four pounds. Compaq sold 53,000 units in its first year and followed up with Mark II and Mark III models, the latter pictured here. Compaq also produced the first desktop IBM clone, the DeskPro, in 1984.

Crucially, though, Compaq had demonstrated how to legally produce an IBM clone, and soon the industry followed. By the end of the Eighties, almost every personal-computer company, with the exception of Apple, had scrapped their proprietary systems and moved into IBM clones. Much later, Compaq merged with Hewlett Packard; the new partnership officially started on 7th May 2002.

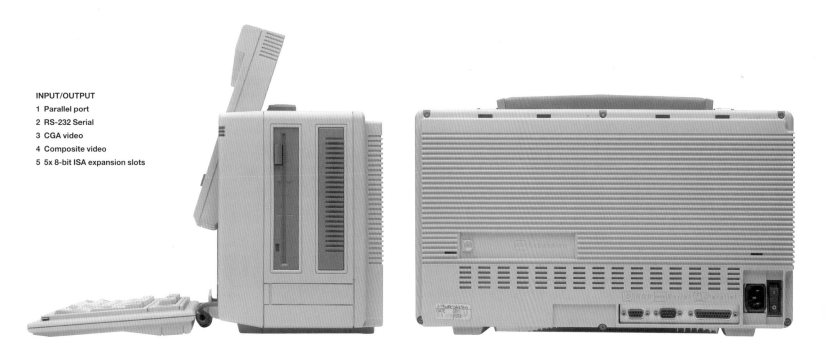

INPUT/OUTPUT

1 Parallel port
2 RS-232 Serial
3 CGA video
4 Composite video
5 5x 8-bit ISA expansion slots

DID YOU KNOW?

Despite setting a US business record of $111.2 million in first-year revenues, Compaq was short on cash. Looking for potential buyers, chairman Ben Rosen actually offered Apple the chance to acquire Compaq for $100 million. Apple chief John Sculley, along with Steve Jobs, turned the offer down, leaving Compaq to grow into one of the biggest IT companies on the planet.

In 1979, Apple proposed three new computers: one would be a successor to the Apple II, the second a technically uncompromising high-end system and the third a home gaming machine. The second became the Lisa, while Jef Raskin was put in charge of the third, which eventually became the Macintosh.

Many believe Steve Jobs got the idea for the graphical user interface (GUI) from a demonstration at Xerox's Palo Alto Research Center (PARC). According to Raskin, though, Jobs took some persuading to even pay a visit.

While the mouse had been invented by Douglas C. Engelbart back in 1963, it was researchers at Xerox PARC who first developed what we'd recognize today as a GUI. PARC opened in 1972, and Raskin was a regular visitor, and at times participant, the following summer. After Raskin became Apple employee number thirty-one in 1978, the Mac and Lisa teams paid a visit to PARC, but apparently Jobs and Wozniak weren't interested in attending.

Raskin and Lisa developer Bill Atkinson believed Jobs should visit PARC in order to share their respective teams' visions, and finally persuaded him to take a tour. Inspired by what he saw, Jobs asked Atkinson how long it would take to produce their own version, unaware the Mac and Lisa teams had already been working on it for seven months.

Apple Lisa

Manufacturer: Apple Computer
Model: Lisa

Launched: January 1983
Country of Origin: USA

COMPANY HISTORY
See **Apple II p21**

SPECIFICATION
CPU model: Motorola 68000
Speed: 5MHz
RAM: 1MB
Special features: Graphical user interface, mouse, built-in 12in monitor, twin floppy drives in Lisa / 3.5in floppy in Lisa 2
Local price at launch: approx $9995

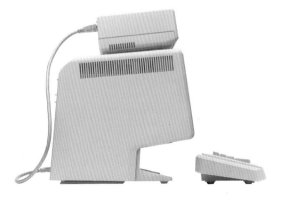

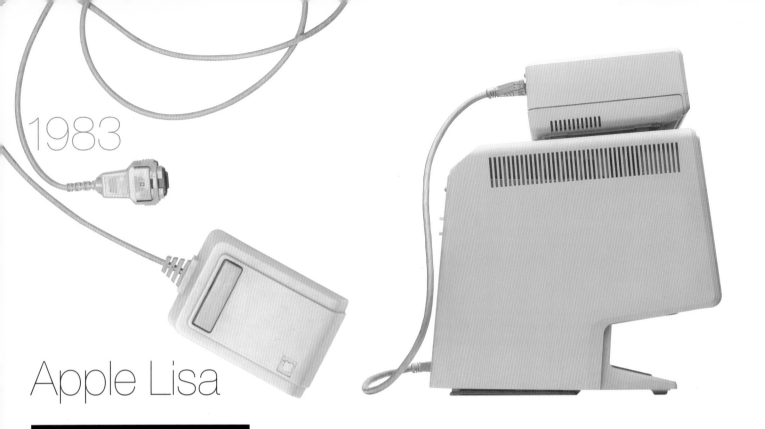

Apple Lisa

120_121

Manufacturer: Apple Computer
Model: Lisa

WHAT HAPPENED NEXT

The Lisa became the first personal computer to employ a graphical user interface, and while Xerox PARC provided much inspiration, Apple introduced several innovations, including the Trash Can. However, the Lisa felt slow and was limited to just seven built-in applications. It was expensive, too, costing around ten times as much as an Apple II. The real nail in Lisa's coffin came a year

later. Back in 1979, Jef Raskin had suggested that Apple's proposed games-system project instead become a general-purpose computer with a graphical interface. This machine was launched in January 1984 as the Macintosh, and it cost a fraction of the Lisa's price. Despite introducing the Lisa 2 in 1984 and later rebranding it as the Macintosh XL, Apple discontinued the line in 1985 in favour of the stronger machine.

This bulky, 48-pound case design prefigured its ignominious future as the housing for the Macintosh XL. It did, however, provide easy access to the two 5.25-inch disc drives (or single 3.5-inch drive that replaced them in the Lisa 2). In essence though, it is very similar in approach to 1977's Tandy TRS-80.

INPUT/OUTPUT

1 2x RS232 serial
2 3x proprietory expansion slots
3 Parallel (on Lisa 1, Lisa 2 pictured)
4 Mouse
5 Video out

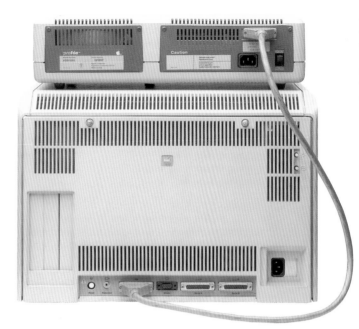

Despite the Lisa's size, the optional 5MB Profile hard disc (later raised to 10MB for the Lisa 2) sat on top of the system, housed in a separate case. It was not an especially elegant solution, given both the machine's price tag and Apple's marketing, which featured the Lisa in stylish Eighties environments.

DID YOU KNOW?

Lisa officially stood for Local Integrated System Architecture, but coincidentally shared the name of Jobs's eldest daughter. The original Lisa's twin floppy drives were also nicknamed Twiggies.

Oric-1

Oric was formed out of Tangerine Computer Systems to exploit the booming home computer market. With backing from British Car Auctions, Oric began development of a machine based on Paul Kaufman's earlier Tangerine Tiger concepts, but aimed squarely at the mass market. While the case, keyboard, memory and pricing would pitch the new machine directly against the likes of Sinclair's ZX Spectrum, the internal specifications were much more impressive.

While most systems of this price exclusively employed RF outputs for TV displays, Oric's machine also offered an RGB monitor interface. It additionally featured a Centronics printer interface as standard, and rather than using the Z80A processor, Oric opted for the 6502A. After the ZX Spectrum's weak beeps, gamers were also delighted to find a powerful General Instruments 8912 sound chip that belted out four channels of audio from a large built-in loudspeaker. The four sound effects, EXPLODE, SHOOT, ZAP and PING could often be heard across busy stores.

The new machine was announced in autumn 1982, but it wasn't officially launched until January the following year. Oric secured deals to supply over 200,000 units to six major UK retailers, promising more power than the Spectrum, but at a lower price. The Oric-1 delivered on both counts, although it only barely undercut the Spectrum at £99.95 and £169.95 for the 16KB and 48KB versions.

| **Manufacturer:** Oric Products International | **Launched:** January 1983 |
| **Name:** Oric-1 | **Country of Origin:** England |

SPECIFICATION
CPU model: 6502A
Speed: 1MHz
RAM: 16 or 48KB
Special features: RGB and Centronics interfaces. Powerful loudspeaker
Local price at launch: £99.95 (16KB), £169.95 (48KB)

COMPANY HISTORY
Oric Products International was formed out of Tangerine Computer Systems in April 1982, the parent company providing research and development. Tangerine itself was originally formed in 1979 by Barry Muncaster and Dr. Paul Johnson, whose first product was the Microtan-65 *(see p50)*. In 1981, Paul Kaufman joined Tangerine, and the following year, the company sold its Tandata Prestel division. Tangerine remained faithful to the Prestel system, though, with Kaufman devising a new machine designed to link directly into it. His proposed system became the blueprint for the Tangerine Tiger, but it was never released. Instead, Tangerine decided to enter the booming entry-level home-computer market under the spin-off brand Oric Products International.

Oric-1

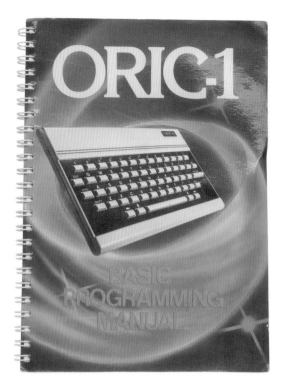

The Oric's design makes it apparent the company was going after Sinclair's market. Unlike the Sinclairs, however, the inevitable array of peripherals – which included a lightpen and a four-colour plotter – did not manage to keep the theme going.

Manufacturer: Oric Products International
Name: Oric-1

WHAT HAPPENED NEXT

Oric may have enjoyed large initial orders, but, like many of its rivals, it had announced its computer long before actual products were available. Worse, its ROM chip suffered from several bugs, which added up to Sinclair significantly outselling the Oric on home turf. It was successfully exported to France, though, where it earned an award for Home Computer of the Year.
In 1984, Oric launched the Atmos for £179. This version essentially fixed the Oric-1's ROM bugs, increased the speed and featured a new case with an improved keyboard. By this time, however, the Spectrum's momentum was unstoppable. Oric later announced plans for three new computers, including the Stratos, which launched on 1st February 1985, but insurmountable debts forced the UK division to go into receivership the following day. The International Branch lasted a little longer in France, even releasing the Telestrat model, but it, too, fell into receivership in 1987.

INPUT/OUTPUT
1 Expansion bus
2 Tape
3 Printer
4 RGB TV

digital : retro

Mattel
Aquarius

During the summer of 1982, Mattel's IntelliVision game console was selling well and was recognized as technologically superior to its archrival, the Atari VCS. However, a failed promise to produce a peripheral had drawn unwanted attention from the FTC and incurred a hefty monthly fine.

Mattel had long promised to launch a keyboard unit for the IntelliVision that would have turned the console into a personal computer – but high costs caused delays, disgruntling customers. The FTC investigated Mattel for fraud and reportedly ordered it to pay a fine of $10,000 per month until the promised keyboard became widely available.

Mattel's hasty response was to release the Entertainment Computer System, ECS, previously developed as a sideline. The FTC was satisfied, but Mattel recognized that the time was right to exploit the booming home computer market. Lacking the time to develop a system, it started looking for an existing system it could rebrand.

Luckily, Radofin Far East, the Hong Kong manufacturer of Mattel's IntelliVision parts, had already developed three computers based on the Z80 processor. Mattel struck a deal to sell two of the models, code-named Checkers and Chess, in the US, and announced them as the Aquarius I and II at the winter 1982 Consumer Electronics Show. The Aquarius I became widely available the following spring.

Manufacturer: Mattel	**Launched:** June 1983
Name: Aquarius	**Country of Origin:** USA

SPECIFICATION

CPU model: Z80
Speed: 3.5MHz
RAM: 4KB
Special features: Same sound chip as IntelliVision console. Launched with numerous peripherals including a Mini-Expander unit that could take hand controllers and two cartridges.
Local price at launch: $160

COMPANY HISTORY

See **Mattel IntelliVision p46**

digital : retro

Mattel
Aquarius

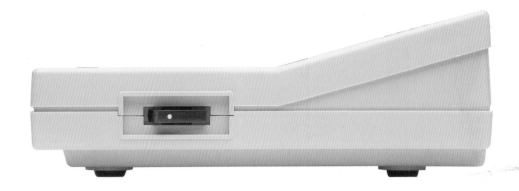

128_129

Manufacturer: Mattel
Name: Aquarius

WHAT HAPPENED NEXT

Mattel now had its own home computer, but it was woefully underpowered, even for 1983. Its 3.5MHz processor was equalled by many earlier models, while only 1.7KB of its mere 4KB memory remained once the supplied Microsoft BASIC Interpreter was running.
The game performance was also disappointing, especially coming three years after the impressive IntelliVision. In fact, game designer Bob Del Principe summed up the feelings of fellow programmers with the slogan "Aquarius – system for the Seventies!" The Aquarius I was sufficiently unsuccessful for Mattel to cancel the Aquarius II summer launch and, by autumn, it had negotiated itself out of its contract with Radofin. The subsequent video-games crash saw Mattel Electronics close its doors in January 1984.

INPUT/OUTPUT
1 Tape (600 baud)
2 RF video
3 Printer (proprietory)
4 Bus

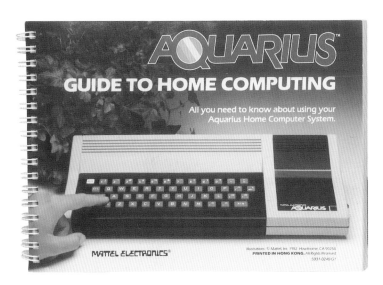

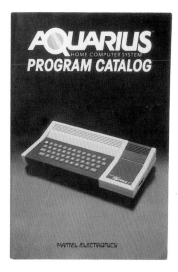

DID YOU KNOW?

One party at Mattel benefited from the Aquarius's quick demise: *Burgertime* became one of IntelliVision's best-known video games, thanks to an unexpectedly large marketing campaign originally intended for the Aquarius. Mattel had booked considerable airtime and ad space for its ill-fated home computer, but devoted it to *Burgertime* when the Aquarius didn't work out. With a lifespan of less than six months from launch to withdrawal, the Aquarius enjoys the dubious honour of being one of the least successful home computers ever.

Nintendo Famicom/ NES

During the late Seventies, Nintendo president Hiroshi Yamauchi called on his games designer Gunpei Yokoi to produce something new. The result was Nintendo's Game and Watch handheld games, which employed flip-open LCD screens and the now-ubiquitous four-way, cross-shaped control pad.

Yokoi was then told to assist recent Nintendo recruit Shigeru Miyamoto on a new arcade project. Inspired by the fairy tale of Beauty and the Beast, Miyamoto devised a platform game in which a huge gorilla kidnaps the girlfriend of a small heroic jumping character. The gorilla was named Kong, with the word Donkey appended to refer to its stubborn nature. *Donkey Kong* was launched in 1981 and became hugely popular.

Yamauchi divided Nintendo's R&D department into four teams and encouraged them to compete against each other. Yokoi, Miyamoto and Masayuki Uemoura headed three, while the fourth concentrated on chips under Takeda Genyo.

Uemoura's R&D2 team worked on Nintendo's debut into the home video-game console market, developing the Family Computer System, or Famicom for short. It launched in Japan on 15th July 1983, and included *Donkey Kong*, *Donkey Kong Jr*. and *Popeye*. Miyamoto later wrote a new platform game featuring his jumping character from *Donkey Kong*, turning him into an Italian plumber called Mario. The *Super Mario Brothers* game became an instant hit and made Miyamoto a legend.

Manufacturer: Nintendo
Name: Famicom / NES (pictured)

Launched: July 1983
Country of Origin: Japan

SPECIFICATION

CPU model: Custom 6502
Speed: 1.78MHz
RAM: 2KB
Special features: *Super Mario Brothers* Game, optional Robotic Operations Buddy for NES version
Local price at launch: ¥14,800 (Yen)

COMPANY HISTORY

Nintendo can be traced back to 1889, when Fusajiro Yamauchi, the great-grandfather of Nintendo's current president, began manufacturing Japanese Hanafuda playing cards in Kyoto. In 1950, Yamauchi's great-grandson Hiroshi took over the reins. During the Sixties, Gunpei Yokoi, a Kyoto local who'd recently graduated in electronics, was taken on to maintain the playing-cards assembly line. In 1970, Yokoi was transferred into Nintendo's growing games department and challenged to produce "something great"

for the Christmas market. Gunpei returned with a mechanical arm toy he'd built for himself. Subsequently launched as the Ultrahand, Nintendo's first toy sold over 1.2 million units. Over the following years, Yokoi's team produced the Ultramachine automatic indoor baseball pitcher and the Ultrascope periscope toy. Yokoi then poached Masayuki Uemoura from Sharp and employed that company's solar cells to produce the first electronic toy in Japan: the Beam Gun. Nintendo followed it in 1973 with laser clay-pigeon shooting.

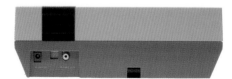

1983

Nintendo Famicom/ NES

Manufacturer: Nintendo
Name: Famicom / NES

WHAT HAPPENED NEXT

After selling 2.5 million Famicoms in Japan, Nintendo felt ready to launch worldwide. It first approached Atari for help with a US launch, but after being turned down, it went ahead alone. In autumn 1985, the Famicom, rebranded as the Nintendo Entertainment System (pictured here), arrived in the US. While many were indifferent to its accompanying Robotic Operating Buddy (ROB), the NES itself flew off the shelves, with Miyamoto's *Legend of Zelda* game becoming the first to sell over a million copies.

The NES enjoyed a long life and was only superseded in 1992 by the Super Famicom/Super NES. Nintendo followed this with the N64 and GameCube in 1996 and 2001, respectively. Hiroshi Yamauchi stepped down in 2002 after fifty-two years at the helm; Miyamoto still heads up the key Mario games.

Where earlier game consoles had looked like stereo systems, taking their cues from Seventies living-room furniture, the NES had more in common with another Eighties arrival, the VCR. Its hidden cartridge-slot mimicked the slot-loading mechanism of most VHS machines, with both system buttons mounted where tape controls might be.

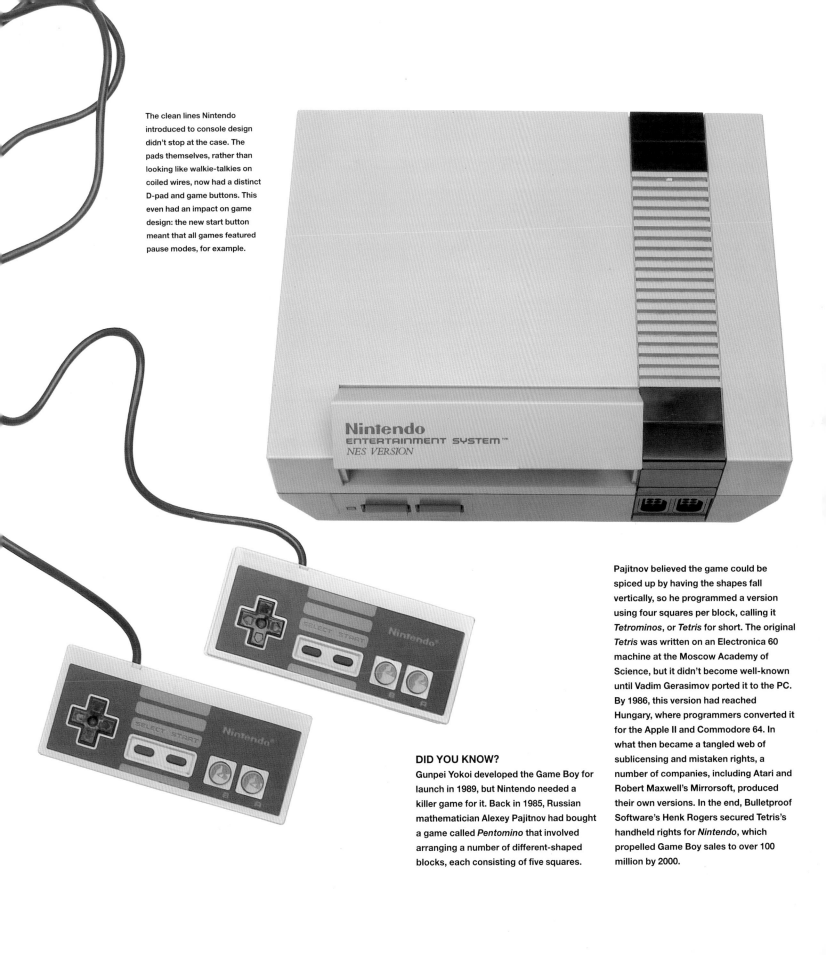

The clean lines Nintendo introduced to console design didn't stop at the case. The pads themselves, rather than looking like walkie-talkies on coiled wires, now had a distinct D-pad and game buttons. This even had an impact on game design: the new start button meant that all games featured pause modes, for example.

Pajitnov believed the game could be spiced up by having the shapes fall vertically, so he programmed a version using four squares per block, calling it *Tetrominos*, or *Tetris* for short. The original *Tetris* was written on an Electronica 60 machine at the Moscow Academy of Science, but it didn't become well-known until Vadim Gerasimov ported it to the PC. By 1986, this version had reached Hungary, where programmers converted it for the Apple II and Commodore 64. In what then became a tangled web of sublicensing and mistaken rights, a number of companies, including Atari and Robert Maxwell's Mirrorsoft, produced their own versions. In the end, Bulletproof Software's Henk Rogers secured Tetris's handheld rights for *Nintendo*, which propelled Game Boy sales to over 100 million by 2000.

DID YOU KNOW?
Gunpei Yokoi developed the Game Boy for launch in 1989, but Nintendo needed a killer game for it. Back in 1985, Russian mathematician Alexey Pajitnov had bought a game called *Pentomino* that involved arranging a number of different-shaped blocks, each consisting of five squares.

When Acorn launched the BBC Micro at the end of 1981, it offered two versions: the cheaper Model A was designed for mass-market appeal, leaving the pricier Model B for enthusiasts who demanded greater memory and expandability. Much to Acorn's surprise, the buying public generally neglected the Model A in favour of the Model B. While the Acorn team was pleased the market had proved sophisticated enough to prefer the Model B, its subsequent price increase to £399 left the company without a compelling product for the exploding entry-level market.

Acorn's solution was to produce a cut-down version of the BBC Model B, but employing more efficient manufacturing and better branding. The new machine had the Model B's 2MHz 6502 processor and 32KB of RAM, but it drove its memory in a more cost-effective manner, dispensed with the BBC's graphics Mode-7 and had one sound voice instead of three. There were fewer ports, too, but inclusion of both TV and RGB video outputs made it more sophisticated than the competition. Combining the video, audio and I/O features into a single custom-built ULA chip reduced manufacturing costs.

Once again in keeping with its physics nomenclature, Acorn named its new machine the Electron and launched it in August 1983 for £199.

Acorn Electron

Manufacturer: Acorn Computers Ltd
Name: Electron

Launched: August 1983
Country of Origin: England

COMPANY HISTORY

See Acorn Atom, p62

SPECIFICATION

CPU model: 6502
Speed: 2MHz
RAM: 32KB
Special features: Custom ULA chip handling video, audio and I/O
Local price at launch: £199

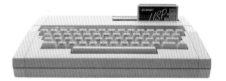

Acorn Electron

Manufacturer: Acorn Computers Ltd
Name: Electron

WHAT HAPPENED NEXT

The Electron's custom ULA was designed to reduce manufacturing costs, but production problems with the chip left Acorn severely understocked for the important 1983 Christmas sales period. Determined not to lose out in 1984, a year in which the market was expected to further expand, Acorn committed to producing large quantities of Electrons.

Contrary to earlier projections, though, the home-computer market was collapsing by the summer of 1984. Demand for new machines plummeted but, infuriatingly for Acorn, the company was locked into producing far more Electrons than it could now hope to sell. Despite a £4 million advertising campaign, many Electrons built were never sold.

INPUT/OUTPUT
1 Expansion port
2 Tape (1200 baud)
3 RF TV out
4 RGB video

digital : retro

The Plus 1 expansion, featured
here, provided two cartridge
slots, a true analogue/digital
joystick port that could also be
used with measuring
instruments and a Centronics
parallel port. Most of the
cartridges Acorn Soft produced
were games.

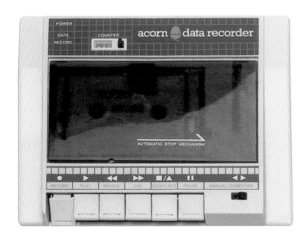

DID YOU KNOW?
The £4 million advertising campaign to
increase sales of the Electron featured
iconic Scottish comedian and
impressionist Stanley Baxter.

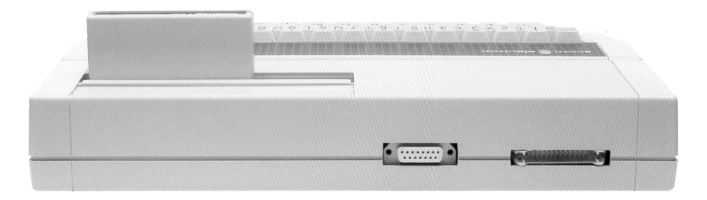

On 16th June 1983, Microsoft announced its MSX specification for 8-bit home computers. Machines conforming to the MSX specification would, theoretically, run the same software – including Microsoft's own MSX BASIC – thereby bringing a level of compatibility to the low-cost market that didn't previously exist.

The name MSX is often said to be short for MicroSoft eXtended or Matsushita Sony X, where X could represent any other company. MSX developer Kazuhiko Nishi is supposed to have jokingly suggested NSX for Nishi Sony X machine but discovered Honda already had a car with the same name. He claims MSX actually stands for Machines with Software eXchangability.

When Microsoft announced MSX , in June 1983, no fewer than twenty-two companies expressed an interest in licensing it. By September, Microsoft had announced MSX-DOS (primarily developed by Tim Patterson), which brought the MS-DOS disk format and user interface to MSX. Toward the end of 1983, the first MSX machines were launched. Yamaha was first out of the gate in October, with Sony following with its HB-75 HitBit in November.

Manufacturer: Sony
Model: HB-75 HitBit

Launched: November 1983
Country of Origin: Japan

MSX HISTORY

The undisputed father of MSX was Kazuhiko Nishi of the ASCII Corporation in Japan, a publishing company that shared a name with – but was unrelated to – the American Standard Code for Information Interchange. Nishi worked with Microsoft to devise a standard hardware and software specification for 8-bit home computers.

To meet the standard, computers would need a Zilog Z80 processor, video and sound chips from Texas Instruments and General Instruments, respectively, a cartridge slot and 32KB ROM containing Microsoft's MSX BASIC, along with the appropriate I/O and graphics subroutines. Manufacturers would also need to license the specification from Microsoft. Numerous MSX machines appeared, virtually all hailing from Japanese manufacturers including Canon, Casio, Fujitsu, Hitachi, JVC, Kyocera, Matsushita, Mitsubishi, NEC, Pioneer and Sanyo. The only non-Japanese companies to sell MSX machines were SpectraVideo and Philips, although even the latter's were built by Kyocera.

SPECIFICATION

CPU model: Z80A
Speed: 3.58MHz
RAM: 64KB
Special features: MSX Standard, MSX BASIC, RGB output
Local price at launch: approx ¥50,000 (Yen)

Sony
HB-75
HitBit

Sony provided a range of accessories for the MSX. In addition to the inevitable printers and cassette drives, it was possible to pick up a branded trackball and even an infrared game-controller.

Manufacturer: Sony
Model: HB-75 HitBit

WHAT HAPPENED NEXT
Microsoft described MSX as a standard base upon which to build different machines with added value, such as supporting audio or video enhancements. This concept, however, proved to be the MSX's undoing.
For example, Yamaha's MSX featured enhanced audio, JVC's could interface with home entertainment systems while

Pioneer's offered video effects and control of an early Laserdisc player. All were exciting enhancements, but the software designed to exploit them broke away from the MSX standard, thereby rendering them as proprietary as their 8-bit competitors. MSX was developed until 1988, with official enhancements including MSX-2, MSX-2+ and TurboR800.

INPUT/OUTPUT
1 2x joystick ports
2 Cartridge slot
3 Tape (1200/2400 baud)
4 RGB video out
5 SCART video out
6 Monitor video out
7 Centronics interface

digital : retro

DID YOU KNOW?

Sony's current CEO, Nobuyuki Idie, was actually general manager of the company's MSX team in 1983. Sony's HB-75 HitBit was not only one of the first MSX machines to be launched, it was one of the best, featuring 64KB RAM, RGB display output and support for their new 3.5-inch floppy drive.

The SpectraVideo SVI-738 Xpress (top) was an MSX-1 variant sold in the US. It had a right-mounted floppy-disk drive, like many computers that followed it, and it was designed to be portable – hence the name Xpress and the bundled carrying case.

The Sanyo MPC-100 (bottom) is a good example of the MSX range's drawbacks. It was a perfectly capable, MSX-1 compatible machine, but with the addition of a lightpen socket. It even had a hole in the top right to rest the pen in, or, alternatively, a badge proudly displaying the RAM.

Apple
Macintosh

When Apple proposed three new systems in 1979, Jef Raskin was asked to head up the home games project. Raskin, however, had other ideas: he'd been thinking about graphical-based computers since the late Sixties. Rather than produce a games machine, Raskin proposed a general-purpose, low-cost computer with a graphical user interface, and was asked to explain his idea in detail.

Raskin began work on his "Book of Macintosh", a technical specification including everything from hardware to software to marketing. Raskin had also already coined a name for his new machine, calling it Macintosh, after his favourite variety of apple.

Burrell Smith built the first Mac prototype and later produced a version employing the Motorola 68000 processor, while Andy Hertzfield adapted much of Bill Atkinson's existing Lisa interface. Raskin, however, resigned in 1982, before the Mac was finished; Steve Jobs took over the project.

When the Macintosh was finally unveiled on 25th January 1984, it was more than just the first affordable computer with a GUI; it was also the first to employ Sony's brand-new 3.5-inch floppy drive, which in Jerry Mannock's case design resembled a friendly smile. The face of personal computing had changed forever.

142_143

Manufacturer: Apple Computer
Name: Macintosh (Plus model pictured)

Launched: January 1984
Country of Origin: USA

SPECIFICATION

CPU model: Motorola 68000
Speed: 8MHz
RAM: 128KB
Special features: Graphical user interface, mouse, built-in 9in screen, 3.5in floppy drive
Local price at launch: $2495

COMPANY HISTORY
See **Apple II p20**

1984

Apple Macintosh

144_145

In contrast to the two-button mouse of the IBM PC, the original Macintosh mouse had only a single button. The design team working on the Mac Plus saw no reason to alter this. Even today, all Macs retain a single-button mouse – although its shape and the way it functions have changed over the years.

Manufacturer: Apple Computer
Name: Macintosh (Plus model pictured)

WHAT HAPPENED NEXT

Everyone agreed the Macintosh was groundbreaking, but it had to wait a year for a killer application. In 1985, Aldus launched PageMaker for the Mac, and CEO Paul Brainerd coined the term desktop publishing. In the same year, Adobe released PostScript, allowing laser printers to act as accurate proofing tools. The combination of Macintosh, PageMaker and PostScript sealed Apple's close relationship with creative publishing, which exists to this day.

Many enhanced Macs were released over the years, including the Mac Plus pictured here. By the early Nineties, though, the upright single-box range had almost entirely been superseded by the more serious Mac II systems, leaving Mac Classics to wrap up the legend. Ironically, Apple's fortunes were later transformed by another single-box computer: the iMac, launched in the late Nineties.

The Mac Plus keyboard was larger than that of the original Mac. For the first time, it featured a numeric keypad. Four new cursor keys also appeared to the right of the Space bar, below the slightly larger Return key. The keyboard only featured one Option and one Command key.

digital : retro

INPUT/OUTPUT

1 Floppy disk drive
   (3.5 in. double-sided 800KB)
2 Keyboard socket
3 Audio jack
4 Mouse port
5 External floppy disk drive port
6 SCSI port – debuted on the Mac Plus
   model
7 Serial printer port
8 Serial modem port
9 Power socket
10 Power switch
11 Battery compartment

DID YOU KNOW?

Apple was already using one of the hottest ad agencies around, which had access to British film director Ridley Scott. Once Scott learned the Macintosh was to be launched in 1984 to a market dominated by faceless IBM, he immediately knew what had to be done.

The result was an award-winning commercial in which a female athlete runs through the nightmarish land of George Orwell's *1984* and swings a sledgehammer through the projection of *Big Brother*.

Remarkably, this commercial was shown only once, during the third-quarter broadcast of the Los Angeles Raiders vs. Washington Redskins Super Bowl. The production cost $500,000, but the prime advertising placement weighed in at a cool million dollars. It paid off: tens of millions of Americans saw the commercial, which made headlines the world over. The Macintosh had arrived to save us from the conformist corporate nightmare of Big Blue IBM.

1984

Sinclair
QL

Buoyed by the success of the ZX Spectrum, Clive Sinclair's next objective was to enter the business market, but he and designer David Karlin had different ideas. Karlin joined Sinclair in 1982 on his return to the UK from Palo Alto, where he'd designed DSP chips for Fairchild.

Karlin's concept was to get as close as possible to the high performance of workstations like the Xerox Star, but using modern technology to achieve a price of just £1,000. Sinclair, on the other hand, considered £400 to be the absolute limit.

With a strict budget monitored by Sinclair himself, the project kicked off with Karlin on electronics and new recruit Tony Tebby on the operating system, leaving Sinclair veteran Rick Dickinson to handle the industrial design – which included a new flat-faced keyboard. The budget would not accommodate a floppy drive, so a pair of Sinclair's MicroDrive tape drives were used.

Psion, which had produced the starter tape for the ZX Spectrum, wrote an application suite consisting of a word processor (Quill), a spreadsheet (Abacus), a business graphics package (Easel) and a database (Archive). To differentiate the new machine from the earlier ZX range, it was called the Quantum Leap, or QL for short.

Manufacturer: Sinclair
Model: QL

Launched: January 1984
Country of Origin: England

SPECIFICATION
CPU model: Motorola 68008
Speed: 8MHz
RAM: 128KB
Special features: 2 x built-in MicroDrive tape units
Local price at launch: £399

COMPANY HISTORY
See **Sinclair ZX80, p58.**

digital : retro

Sinclair QL

Manufacturer: Sinclair
Model: QL

INPUT/OUTPUT

1 2x RS232 serial
2 2x Sinclair Network
3 2x Controller
4 ROM connector
5 Expansion bus
6 External MicroDrives bus
7 RGB video out
8 RF video out

WHAT HAPPENED NEXT

The QL was launched in January 1984 with a great deal of confidence; its TV ad featured the recently knighted Sir Clive Sinclair taking an enormous leap over his competitors' machines. To be fair, the QL had a lot going for it: the hardware was impressive for the price, while its preemptive multitasking capabilities weren't matched by PCs until around ten years later. Sadly for the QL, though, it suffered from many technical and production problems, including unreliable MicroDrives, an unfinished ROM on early models and the familiar Sinclair delays. With the IBM PC gaining momentum, the QL's timing was wrong, and the system gradually disappeared.

Much is made of the flaws of Sinclair's MicroDrives, but they also presented significant advantages. They were a compact, elegant solution for the need to speed up data access without the cost of a disk drive – though they were accessed far too frequently by the original version of the Psion applications suite.

DID YOU KNOW?

The QL was well-known for its excellent programming facilities, which encouraged many to further develop their skills. One such QL user was a young Finn who gave up his Commodore VIC-20 for the new Sinclair machine. He learned assembly language and wrote a number of programs on his QL before upgrading to a 386 PC, on which he wrote a cut-down version of the UNIX operating system. The young man was called Linus Torvalds, and he nicknamed his new operating system Linux.

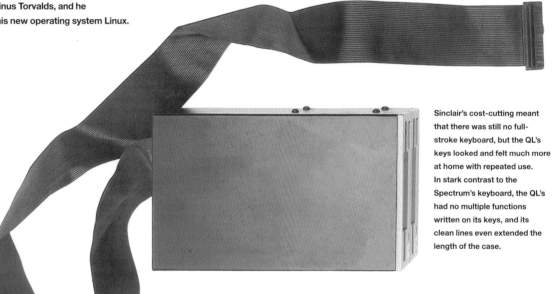

Sinclair's cost-cutting meant that there was still no full-stroke keyboard, but the QL's keys looked and felt much more at home with repeated use. In stark contrast to the Spectrum's keyboard, the QL's had no multiple functions written on its keys, and its clean lines even extended the length of the case.

Amstrad CPC-464

Amstrad founder Alan Sugar had a clear idea of what his company's first home computer should be. He described typical Amstrad customers as truck drivers making impulse purchases on wet Sunday afternoons. These customers believed they knew what computers should look like from visiting places like travel agents – and they weren't the "pregnant calculators" from rival Sinclair.

Consequently, Sugar demanded a full-size keyboard and a dedicated monitor. Applying earlier manufacturing strategies, his machine would also be a highly integrated unit with a built-in tape drive and a single power supply. Sugar then set Amstrad's technical director and production engineer Bob Watkins to work.

While Watkins's department took care of the case, display and tape drive, the actual circuit board and software were outsourced to a pair of external contractors. They developed a 6502-based system, but then abandoned it halfway. In August 1983, Watkins approached long-term collaborator Ambit to finish the job; the only catch was, he needed it in three months.

Lacking 6502 expertise, Ambit's Roland Perry realized the only way the machine could be built in time was to start from scratch with a more familiar processor: the Z80. So Perry hired school friend and Z80 expert Mark Eric Jones of MEJ Electronics to design the hardware, and Locomotive to write the software.

Manufacturer: Amstrad	**Launched:** March 1984
Model: CPC-464	**Country of Origin:** England

SPECIFICATION

CPU model: Z80
Speed: 4MHz
RAM: 64KB
Special features: Built-in tape drive. Machine sold with dedicated monitor.
Local price at launch: £249 (with B&W monitor), £359 (with colour monitor)

COMPANY HISTORY

Amstrad was founded in 1968 by Alan Sugar, and the company name was derived from a shortened version of Alan Michael Sugar Trading. Sugar began business by selling electrical goods like car stereos in London's East End. Amstrad's first venture into manufacturing started in 1970, with hi-fis, and Sugar had a clear idea of how to reduce costs and undercut his rivals. First, rather than use expensive vacuum forming for plastic case parts, he used cheaper injection mouldings.

Second, he adopted the concept of all-in-one hi-fi systems, which saved money by using a single power supply – rather than having one in each component. Serious audiophiles may have balked at such cost-saving exercises, but the low-cost products proved attractive to the general public. As the 1970s drew to a close, Amstrad boasted 50% of the UK tower hi-fi market. As a large electronics company, it was only a matter of time before Amstrad launched a home computer.

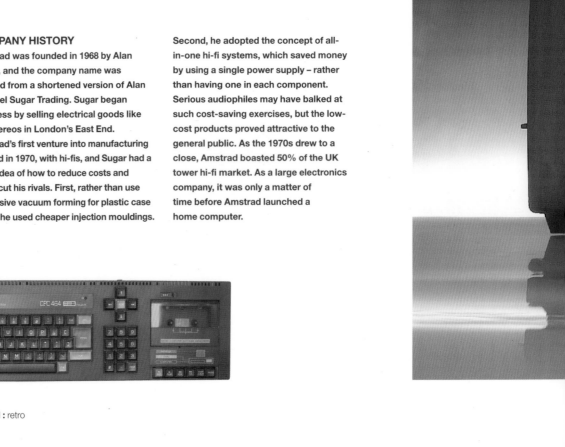

Amstrad
CPC-464

INPUT/OUTPUT
1 Printer port
2 Bus port
3 Joystick
4 Floppy-disc port
5 DIN for monitor
6 Headphone jack

Manufacturer: Amstrad
Model: CPC-464

WHAT HAPPENED NEXT

The prototype met the early December 1983 deadline and was launched in March 1984, with the choice of either a monochrome or colour monitor. Amstrad called it the CPC-464: CPC was short for Colour Personal Computer, and 464 referred to its 64KB of RAM, with a 4 thrown in to avoid confusion with the Commodore 64. The CPC-464 was a success in Europe with several successors – including the 664, which swapped the tape drive for a three-inch floppy drive, and the 6128, which sported 128KB RAM and ran CPM. Amstrad later launched an all-in-one word-processing unit called the PCW *(see p170)*.

Amstrad marketed the CPC-464's completeness. Building in the tape recorder and bundling a matching monitor and big software package helped the machine compare favourably with the Commodore 64, striking a chord with many buyers.

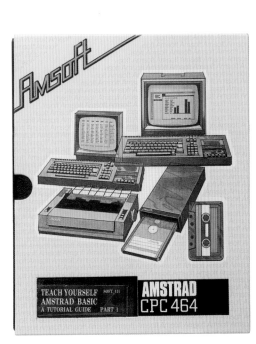

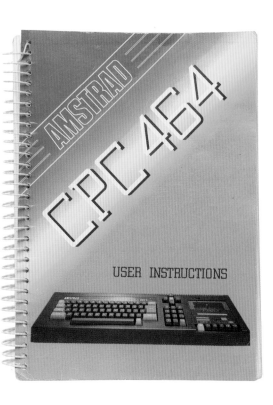

digital : retro

Two years after launching its 5150 Personal Computer, IBM released the 5160 PC XT, short for Extended Technology. This employed the same Intel 8088 processor but featured a minimum of 128KB RAM and a hard disk; the Model 370 boasted 768KB RAM and a 10MB disk for $9000. While it was the first computer of its class to feature a hard disk, the PC XT was essentially just an upgraded version of the 1981 PC.

IBM's Personal Computer team was, however, working on a new architecture it would call AT, or Advanced Technology. Mark Dean – who'd originally joined IBM in 1979 and developed the PC's Colour Graphics Adapter and ISA (Industry Standard Architecture) bus – became the chief engineer of the AT project.

The AT employed Intel's 16-bit 80286 processor running at 6MHz. Dean's team developed a 16-bit extension to his earlier ISA bus, and completed the specification with 256KB RAM, a 1.2MB 5.25-inch floppy-disk drive and optional hard disk. The machine also employed a new 101-key keyboard and ran Microsoft's latest version of DOS. IBM launched the 5170 PC AT on 14th August 1984.

IBM 5170 PC AT

Manufacturer: IBM
Model: 5170 PC AT

Launched: August 1984
Country of Origin: USA

COMPANY HISTORY
See IBM Personal Computer, p78

SPECIFICATION
CPU model: Intel 80286
Speed: 6MHz
RAM: 256KB
Special features: BASIC in ROM, CMOS backup battery, 9-foot coiled keyboard cable
Local price at launch: $3,995

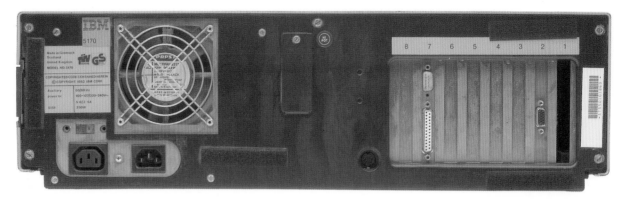

IBM 5170
PC AT

Input/output
1 6x 16-bit ISA slots
2 2x 8-bit ISA slots
3 RS232c serial
4 Centronics parallel
5 Monitor

Manufacturer: IBM
Model: 5170 PC AT

WHAT HAPPENED NEXT

By the time IBM launched the AT, its personal computer range had effectively become the corporate standard. As before, the AT was cloned, further cementing its standard while increasing the wealth of Intel and Microsoft.

The AT would, however, be the last time IBM defined a PC standard others would clone blindly. While IBM later tried to license the MicroChannel Architecture of its PS/2 machines, more popular and economical evolutions emerged from the clones themselves.

Compaq developed a new expansion bus and even beat IBM to ship the first PC based on Intel's new 32-bit 80386 processor. By the early Nineties, Intel had become the dominant player in evolving the PC architecture.

IBM may have created the standard, but it was the clones that propelled it to world domination, in turn making Bill Gates the richest man on the planet.

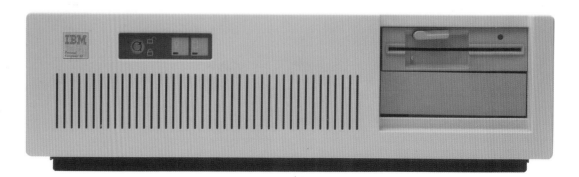

Despite evolutions in home-computer design, the PC AT had much in common with the original 5150 PC, right down to the rounded keyboard back and the angled vertical ventilation grooves on the front of the case.

DID YOU KNOW?

Modern PCs may feature exponentially faster processors and greater storage capabilities, but the desire for backwards-compatibility means that a surprising number of original PC AT design aspects remain today. The processors may now employ extended instruction sets, but they still house the core set from the original 80286, theoretically allowing them to run old software.

The keyboards we use today are still in the layout first introduced back in 1984, despite the fact that a number of keys are now virtually redundant. DOS may seem like a distant memory, but Windows still uses the letters A and C to describe the first floppy- and hard-disk drives, respectively. Perhaps most surprising of all, the PC AT's ancient 16-bit ISA expansion slots were still found in PCs being built as recently as 2000.

Tatung Einstein TC-01

As the home-computer market exploded in the early Eighties, Tatung UK boss Dr. W. T. Lin wanted a piece of the action. He assembled a small team with Roy Clarke as department head, Julian Rangely as project leader and Nigel Deakin and David Wess in charge of software development. A fifth engineer handled the hardware while making use of Tatung's existing PCB layout and mechanical-design resources.

The Tatung computer used the popular Z80A processor running at 4MHz with 80KB of RAM, 16KB of which was devoted to the display. Outputs for a standard TV or RGB monitor were provided, along with both serial and Centronics printer ports, a pair of joystick connectors and the exclusive Tatung Pipe, which accessed the 8-bit data bus. The system included a standard three-inch floppy-disk drive, and offered the option of a second drive – impressive, considering the price.

Industrial designer John Law was responsible for the product styling, which integrated the keyboard and processor units. One of Law's patents included a rectangular depression moulded into the top of the case. The monitor's base was designed to sit in this depression, placing the monitor at optimum viewing distance.

While early development took place in Tatung's laboratory in Bradford, the actual unit went into production at factory headquarters in Telford, near Birmingham.

Manufacturer: Tatung UK
Name: Einstein TC-01

Launched: October 1984
Country of Origin: England

SPECIFICATION
CPU model: Z80A
Speed: 4MHz
RAM: 80KB
Special features: Built-in 3in floppy disk drive, depression in case to position monitor
Local price at launch: £499

COMPANY HISTORY
Tatung was founded by Mr. Shan-Chih Lin in 1918, and was named after an old district in Taiwan's capital, Taipei. The company's first documented milestone came in 1939, when the Tatung Iron Works was established. In 1946, Tatung repaired 577 railway cars for postwar Taiwan, and by the end of the decade, it had begun specializing in high-quality electric fans. During the Sixties, Tatung moved into producing refrigerators, TVs and air-conditioning units, and set up a vocational school that later evolved into the Tatung Institute of Technology. As the company grew, it offered scholarships and internships to students of its university. Tatung's involvement with IT began in 1973, with the opening of the Tatung Chinese Character Processing Computer Company. During the Seventies, Tatung opened branches in Japan and America, and in 1981 it established its UK office. While Tatung UK started supplying TVs, VCRs, monitors and domestic after-sales support, it would later design and launch its own home computer.

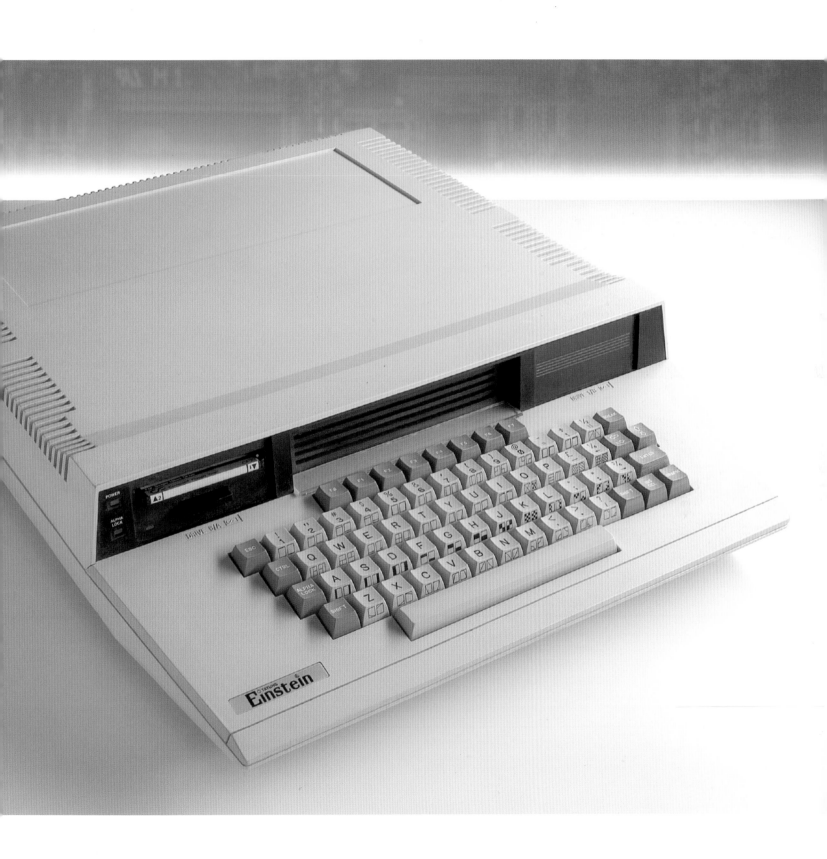

Tatung Einstein TC-01

Manufacturer: Tatung UK
Name: Einstein TC-01

WHAT HAPPENED NEXT

The Einstein may have been technically impressive and described as a dream by some programmers, but its price and specification fell uncomfortably between typical home and business computers. While Tatung launched an Einstein user magazine and wrote software for the machine, few third parties were interested in developing for it. It was too expensive for a home computer, and it lacked the power and software demanded by business users. Tatung later launched an expanded 256KB Einstein, but by this time, it had acquired the rights to produce IBM PC clones.

INPUT/OUTPUT

1 RS232c serial
2 Centronics
3 User port
4 2x joystick
5 Bus Z80
6 RGB TV

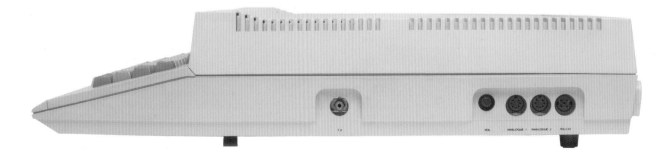

digital : retro

The size and weight of the
Einstein case derived from the
built-in PSU and its ability to
support a monitor, in a similar
manner to the Apple II.

DID YOU KNOW?

Tatung originally wanted to name its
machine after a fruit, but with Apple,
Tangerine and Apricot already taken, the
company couldn't decide on a suitable
alternative. After much debate, Einstein
was chosen to inspire confidence in its
"technical genius".

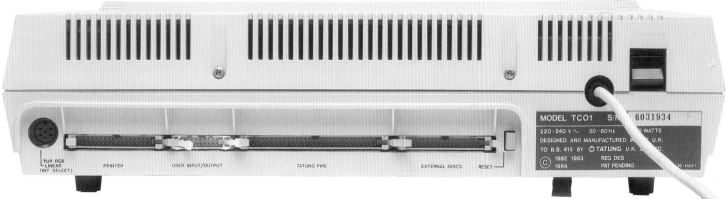

Atari
520ST
/1040ST

During the summer of 1983, Commodore boss Jack Tramiel started an aggressive price war with Texas Instruments, forcing it to quit the home-computer market. This strategy, however, hit Commodore's profits hard and sufficiently upset its board of directors to vote Tramiel out in January 1984. Tramiel subsequently started Tramiel Technologies, which, on 2nd July 1984, bought Atari's Home Computing division from Warner Communications. He moved in with his three sons, their wives and a loyal group of former Commodore employees.

Before Tramiel's takeover, Atari had loaned the cash-strapped Amiga company $500,000 as part of a deal to license its custom chips. Tramiel's team had, however, begun work on a 16-bit machine it believed to be superior. Following brief but complex legal action between Atari, Commodore and Amiga, the Amiga chipset was sold to Commodore, leaving Atari to continue development of its own 16-bit design.

Work really kicked off in September 1984 with former Commodore engineer Shiraz Shivji in charge of hardware. His small team, which included Doug Renn, John Horton, John Hoenig and Jim Tittsler, initially considered National Semiconductor's 32-bit processors, but they secured a better deal on Motorola's 68000. Jack Tramiel's son Leonard was VP of software, while John Feagans, another CBM veteran, worked with Digital Research to port CP/M and the GEM graphical user interface from the PC. Ira Velinsky designed the case.

Manufacturer: Atari	**Launched:** January 1985
Name: 520ST / 1040ST	**Country of Origin:** USA

SPECIFICATION

CPU model: Motorola 68000
Speed: 8MHz
RAM: 512KB (520ST), 1MB (1040ST)
Special features: GEM graphical user interface, MIDI ports
Local price at launch: $799 (520ST), $999 (1040ST)

COMPANY HISTORY

See **Atari VCS, p24 and Commodore PET, p16**

Atari 520ST /1040ST

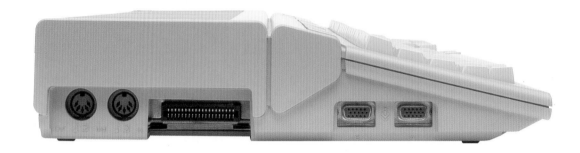

164_165

Manufacturer: Atari
Name: 520ST / 1040ST

WHAT HAPPENED NEXT

Tramiel's slogan "power without the price" was justified for the ST range. It offered 16-bit processing and a graphical interface, with mouse, for much less than its archrival, the Commodore Amiga, or Apple's Macintosh. Soon after the 520ST's launch came the 1MB 1040ST, followed by versions sporting RF modulators for TV connectivity. Next came the Mega ST range with detachable keyboards, up to 4MB RAM, an optional 20MB MegaFile hard disk and the SLM804 laser printer. Atari followed these with the portable STacy, weighing fifteen pounds, and the TT030 (with a 32MHz 68030, SCSI and Ethernet) before announcing the ATW800 Transputer Workstation with INMOS. Come 1992, Atari wound up its computer range with the Falcon 030, a 16MHz system featuring hard-disk audio recording in a conventional 1040ST case.

INPUT/OUTPUT

1 RGB
2 TV modulator
3 Cartridge
4 Midi in
5 Midi out
6 Centronics
7 RS232c serial
8 Hard disk
9 2x joystick
10 Floppy disk
11 Modem
12 Audio (L&R)

digital : retro

DID YOU KNOW?

Early on, the ST carved two specialist niches. Thanks to Shiraz Shivji fitting a pair of MIDI ports as standard, it found itself used for music sequencing in many recording studios. Secondly, while many people exclusively associate Eighties desktop publishing with Macs, the ST proved to be a compelling budget option: after all, for the price of an Apple or IBM laser printer alone, you could buy the Atari laser with a Mega ST and 20MB hard disk. It goes without saying that the ST played great games. Jez San's *Starglider 1* and *2* were 3D classics of their day, while adventures *Guild of Thieves* and *The Pawn* proved photorealistic graphics were possible.

The Atari's case design – incorporating a standard PC-style keyboard, a 3.5-inch disk drive in the right side and the majority of ports at the rear – was not unique, but it set the standard for the last generation of pre-PC computers, including its rival, the Amiga.

Commodore Amiga 1000

In autumn 1982, Jay Miner took former Atari colleague Joe Decuir on a boating trip up the Sacramento River and pitched his plan to develop a new high-end custom chipset. Decuir subsequently joined as badge number three, and the pair started work on project Lorraine, named after Amiga boss Dave Morse's wife.

Miner's team at Atari had previously devised a three-part custom chipset for the earlier 400 and 800 computers, with the goal of easing the load off the main processor. The same strategy would be employed for project Lorraine, and Miner's expanding team, which now included Dave Needle, set to work. At the same time, Morse developed a second side to the business, manufacturing joysticks for Atari machines.

Almost two years later, Miner's team had completed the three custom chips: Agnus, Denise and Paula, handling DMA and the bit-blitter, video output and I/O with audio, respectively. The only question was, what kind of machine would Lorraine be? Miner wanted a high-end, slot-based computer, but Morse and the investors were after a low-cost gaming machine.

Unfortunately, the home-computer market began to collapse, killing the joystick part of the company. Work continued on Lorraine, but Amiga was losing money, with employees remortgaging their homes to keep it afloat. After searching for investors, Amiga received a loan from Atari, who intended to use the new chips in its own computers.

Manufacturer: Commodore	**Launched:** July 1985
Model: Amiga 1000 (A500 pictured)	**Country of Origin:** USA

SPECIFICATION

CPU model: Motorola 68000
Speed: 7.16MHz
RAM: 256KB
Special features: Stereo sound, colour graphical user interface, three custom co-processors
Local price at launch: $1295

COMPANY HISTORY

Amiga was founded in 1982, but its story began at Atari several years earlier, when a team led by Jay Miner developed the 400 and 800 computers. Miner wanted to develop a competitor for the Apple II based on the Motorola 68000 processor and a new custom chipset, but Atari wasn't interested. Miner resigned in 1979 and began designing pacemaker chips for Zimast.

In 1982, Miner was contacted by former colleague Larry Kaplan, who'd left Atari to form Activision. Kaplan was interested in starting a new games company, so Miner introduced Kaplan to his boss at Zimast, who knew potential investors. Hi-Toro was subsequently born, the plan being for Miner to design the chips Zimast would manufacture, leaving Larry to write the games. Dave Morse was recruited from Tonka Toys to be CEO.

Kaplan eventually grew impatient with progress and resigned, so Morse persuaded Miner to replace him as vice president in mid-1982. In order to avoid confusion with the Japanese lawnmower firm Toro, the company also renamed itself Amiga, Spanish for female friend.

1985

Commodore
Amiga

168_169

Manufacturer: Commodore
Model: Amiga 1000 (A500 pictured)

INPUT/OUTPUT

1 Centronics
2 RS232
3 Mouse
4 2x joystick
5 RGB video
6 Composite video
7 Audio (L&R)
8 Bus
9 Disk drive

WHAT HAPPENED NEXT

In July 1984, former Commodore boss Jack Tramiel bought Atari and discovered the earlier loan to Amiga. Following legal action between several parties, Commodore bought Amiga in August and paid its debts, while Atari continued developing its own 16-bit ST computer.

With Commodore's backing, many improvements were made, and eleven months later, the Amiga 1000 launched.

With its custom hardware and Intuition graphical interface (by R.J. Mical), it was considerably more powerful than its 16-bit rival from Atari.

It was also more expensive. In an attempt to compete at the lower end, Commodore later launched the cheaper A500 model. This was followed by the A2000, the first of several higher-end models whose support for video made them perfect for use in many post-production facilities.

This Amiga 500's styling and two joystick ports placed it squarely in the home. The Amiga had the revolutionary ability to draw all its 4,096 colours onscreen at once, though in reality, this "HAM" mode was rarely used for anything other than stills.

DID YOU KNOW?
Commodore launched the Amiga 1000 with much fanfare at Lincoln Center, in New York City, on 23rd July 1985. To demonstrate the Amiga's powerful graphics, Commodore invited Andy Warhol to draw a portrait of Blondie singer Debbie Harry at the event. Coincidentally, Steve Jobs had, one year earlier, presented a Macintosh to Warhol, who seemed impressed by its graphics capabilities.

Jay Miner has commented that one of his favourite aspects of working at Amiga in the early days was being allowed to take his cockapoo, Mitchy, to the office. Mitchy later gained underground fame by having her paw print moulded on the inside of the Amiga 1000's case, alongside the computer's other named designers – an idea borrowed from the first Mac. Mitchy was well-known at Amiga and Atari, where she wore a photo ID badge and had a nameplate on Miner's office door.

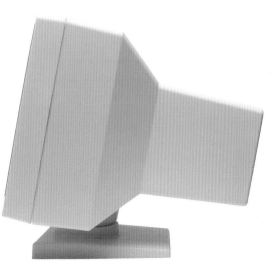

In the mid-Eighties, Amstrad founder and chairman Alan Sugar recognized demand for a low-priced typewriter replacement. Legend has it he sketched his idea of an all-in-one system with built-in portrait monitor and printer on an airplane napkin while flying to Amstrad suppliers in the Far East.

Back in the UK, the project was managed by Roland Perry, who had earlier brought the CPC-464 to market *(see p150)* and was now a full-time employee at Amstrad. Sugar's original idea for a portrait monitor was rejected as being too expensive, and the built-in printer idea was also scrapped and replaced by a separate dot-matrix model. Despite the fact that their machine now resembled a traditional PC, Sugar and Perry constantly reminded the team that they were not building a computer but a dedicated, easy-to-use word-processing system. Rather than use the traditional PC display of 16 lines by 64 characters, for example, Perry advocated a 25-line-by-80-character system that would be better for viewing an entire letter. The custom keyboard also featured keys for cut, copy, paste and print. To keep costs down, a huge custom ASIC chip was created by MEJ Electronics, who'd earlier developed the hardware for the CPC-464. Locomotive also returned to develop custom software and applications, including the Locoscript word processor. The CP/M operating system was added at the eleventh hour.

Amstrad PCW 8256

Manufacturer: Amstrad
Name: PCW 8256 (9512 pictured)

Launched: September 1985
Country of Origin: England

COMPANY HISTORY

See Amstrad CPC-464 p150

SPECIFICATION

CPU model: Z80
Speed: 3.4MHz
RAM: 256KB
Special features: Built-in monitor, custom keyboard and 3in floppy-disk drive. Also sold with printer
Local price at launch: £399

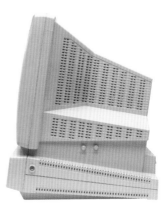

1985

Amstrad PCW

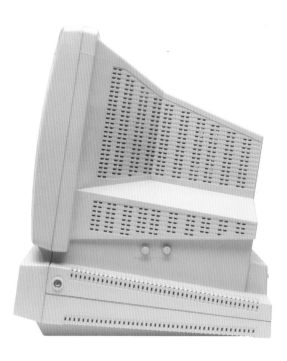

The PCW inspired a certain devotion in its users by making simple word-processing available at an affordable price. The subsequent 9512 model's design, however, hints at greater aspirations; the original 8256 did not include the mock gap between the lower half and the monitor.

Manufacturer: Amstrad
Name: PCW

WHAT HAPPENED NEXT

The Amstrad PCW 8256 was launched at the 1985 Personal Computer World show in London's Olympia exhibition hall for just £399. Many criticized its 3-inch floppy drive, but 3.5-inch models were prohibitively expensive at the time, and most PCs employed prehistoric 5.25-inch floppies instead. Despite claims to the contrary, Amstrad's 3-inch drive was always IBM compatible, and could easily be driven by a standard PC floppy controller.

The PCW was a huge hit with authors and students, selling over one million units during its lifespan. The 8256 was followed by the 8512 and 9512 (pictured here), which came with a daisy-wheel printer. The product line ended with 1998's PCW-16.

INPUT/OUTPUT (8256 and 9512)

1 Z80 bus
2 Parallel
3 Proprietary printer

DID YOU KNOW?

The PCW project was originally code-named Joyce after Sugar's secretary, but when the time came for a commercial name, several alternatives were suggested. MEJ Electronics and Locomotive came up with Zircon and a somewhat convoluted explanation: both companies were originally spun off from Data Recall, which, during the Seventies, produced a departmental word-processing system called the Diamond. Zircon was suggested because the material was a diamond substitute. It was rejected, and a good thing, too, given the impending Zircon spy-satellite scandal. Preferring a more obvious name, Sugar suggested the Word Processing Computer, or WPC for short, but Perry argued people would joke about female police officers. Consequently, Sugar rearranged the initials, coming up with PCW instead.

By the early Eighties, Sega had enjoyed success both in the arcades and with several conversions for existing games consoles, so it was inevitable that the company would enter the home video-game market with its own console.

Sega first dipped its toes with the SG-1000 console, test-marketed in Japan in 1981 and formally launched in June 1983. Sega also offered a home-computer version, complete with built-in keyboard, called the SC-3000. The optional SF-7000 extension added extra memory, a floppy drive and serial and parallel ports. An upgraded SC-3000H version was available later.

Sega followed the SG-1000 with the SG-1000 Mark II game console in 1984, and then the Mark III in 1985. This time, though, Sega had launched to compete with Nintendo's Famicom, which had become enormously popular since its release in 1983.

With a Z80A processor running at 3.6MHz, 8KB of RAM and 16KB of video memory, Sega's Mark III boasted a faster chip, greater memory and more colours than its competitor. It also featured a pair of media slots, allowing it to take either fully featured cartridges or cards with smaller, cheaper games. Sega additionally introduced optional 3D glasses for use with certain games.

1985

Sega
SG-1000
Mark III
Master
System

174_175

Manufacturer: Sega
Model: SG-1000 Mark III / Master System (pictured)

Launched: October 1985
Country of Origin: Japan

COMPANY HISTORY

Sega was officially formed in Japan in May 1952, but its roots can be traced back to Honolulu, Hawaii. There, in 1940, Martin Bromely, Irving Bromberg and James Humpert founded Standard Games. Spotting an opportunity to supply coin-operated games and jukeboxes to US military units stationed in Japan, Bromely suggested a move to Tokyo in 1951. The following year, the company registered a new name: Service Games of Japan, or Sega for short. A year later, American entrepreneur David Rosen formed Rosen Enterprises. Rosen had moved to Tokyo

after serving in the US Air Force in World War II. Rosen Enterprises imported coin-operated machines from the US – instant-photo booths proving the most popular. In 1965, Rosen Enterprises merged with Sega, and one year later, the company launched *Periscope*, a mechanical submarine game. As the decade drew to a close in 1969, Sega was sold to Gulf and Western Industries, with Rosen continuing as CEO. Later in 1979, Rosen and Japanese entrepreneur Hayao Nakayama bought Sega's Japanese assets. Nakayama became CEO, and Rosen headed up the US subsidiary.

SPECIFICATION

CPU model: Z80A
Speed: 3.6MHz
RAM: 8KB
Special features: Two media slots for cartridges or cheaper game cards, optional 3D glasses
Local price at launch: ¥15,000 (Yen)

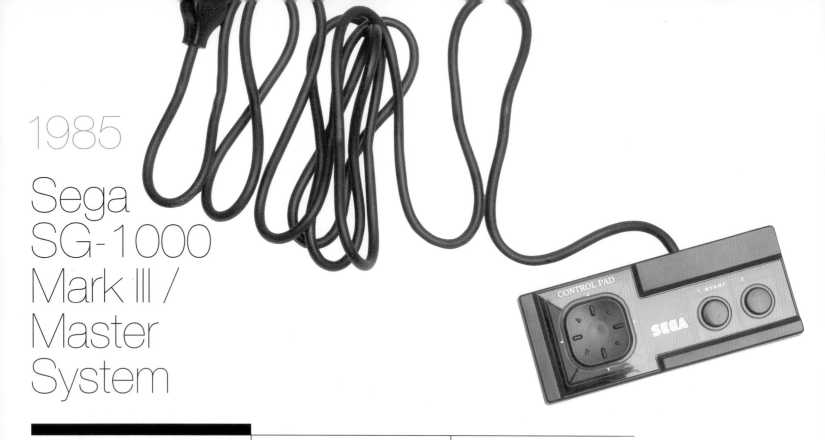

1985

Sega SG-1000 Mark III / Master System

Manufacturer: Sega
Model: SG-1000 Mark III / Master System (pictured)

The Master System had a hidden, built-in game called *The Snail Maze Game*. It could be accessed by turning on the console without a cartridge and pressing up on the D pad and buttons 1 and 2 simultaneously.

WHAT HAPPENED NEXT

While the Mark III was a technically superior machine, Nintendo's Famicom had enjoyed a head start, and Sega struggled to catch up. Nintendo also beat Sega to the US market, rebranding its Famicom as the NES in 1985. Sega repackaged the Mark III as the Master System (pictured here) for its 1986 US launch but, by this time, Nintendo held 90 percent of the market.

Not wanting to be left behind, Sega beat Nintendo to launching the first 16-bit console with its MegaDrive, announced in Japan in 1988 and later released in the US as the Genesis. Sega followed this with the Saturn and Dreamcast consoles launched in Japan in 1994 and 1998, respectively, but competition from the likes of Sony's PlayStation forced the company out of the console hardware market in 2001.

The instructions on the front of the console direct users to the games built in on ROM. These varied, but they could be accessed by turning on the console without inserting a cartridge into the slot.

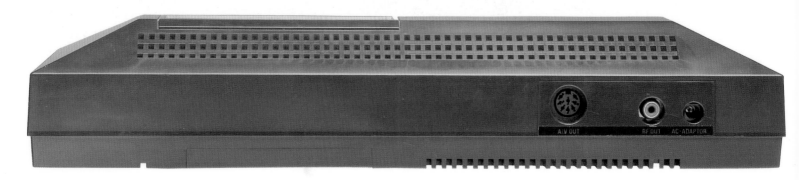

digital : retro

The sharply angular Master System was a child of its time, and as it aged in markets where the Master System was still selling, like Europe, a revised edition (Master System II) with either *Alex Kidd* in *Miracle World* or *Sonic the Hedgehog* included in ROM.

DID YOU KNOW?

As Sega developed the 16-bit Genesis/MegaDrive console, it challenged its top games programmers to come up with a rival for Nintendo's immensely popular Mario character. A team that included Naota Oshima and Yuji Naka responded with Sonic, a speedy hedgehog with running shoes and bright blue, hairlike spines. Sega may have since pulled out of the console hardware market, but it continues writing games, including versions of Sonic for numerous platforms such as XBox, PlayStation 2 and Nintendo's GameCube and GameBoy Advance.

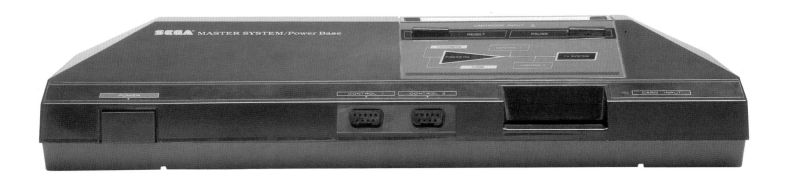

Acorn Archimedes

Back in spring 1983, as Acorn prepared Electron, the company began evaluating processors for its next computer. The research team was unimpressed by Intel's 80286, Motorola's 68000 and National's 16032, believing performance was influenced by memory speed, not just processor speed. Sophie Wilson, programmer of BBC BASIC and designer of the original System-1, wondered if Acorn could develop its own processor, and started toying with a new instruction set. Wilson was inspired by articles sent to her on RISC (Reduced Instruction Set Chip) emerging from a small team of graduates in Berkeley and Palo Alto, California. Designing microprocessors traditionally carried a certain mystique, but when Wilson and long-term Acorn collaborator Steve Furber visited Acorn's 6502 supplier in the US, they found a cottage industry working out of a bungalow. They realized they could make their own microprocessor and returned to convince Acorn boss Hermann Hauser. Hauser was very supportive, and eighteen months later, the first Acorn RISC machine, the ARM processor, was completed. Wilson drafted the instruction set and wrote the BASIC, Furber designed the microarchitecture, while a team that included Tudor Brown and Mike Muller worked on the accompanying chipset, which handled video, memory and I/O. The heart of the future Archimedes computer had been born.

Manufacturer: Acorn Computers	**Launched:** August 1987
Name: Archimedes	**Country of Origin:** England

SPECIFICATION

CPU model: ARM-2 32-bit RISC
Speed: 8MHz
RAM: 512KB (A305) to 16MB (A540)
Special features: GEM graphical
user interface, MIDI ports
Local price at launch: From £799
(A305 model)

COMPANY HISTORY

See **Acorn Atom, p62**

1987

Acorn's operating system used a three-button mouse: The left button, Select, was for working and moving files, and the middle Menu button called context-sensitive menus. There were no drop-down menus. The right button, Adjust, was used to provide opposites – say, an eraser in a graphics program.

Acorn
Archimedes

180_181

Manufacturer: Acorn Computers Ltd
Name: Archimedes

WHAT HAPPENED NEXT

Hauser's original plan for an Office Automation system (a popular concept in the mid-Eighties) was later scrapped, although, fortunately, the ARM chipset had been designed to be very flexible. Acorn began work on a new platform, and a team of programmers led by Paul Fellows developed its initial Arthur operating system. This was later replaced with RISC OS led by William Stoye.

The Archimedes was subsequently launched in August 1987 in three series (300, 400 and 500), offering varying memory and hard-disk configurations. With a team of twenty or so engineers, Acorn had jumped from 8-bit computing to its own 32-bit RISC chip, which today (as **StrongARM**) is widely licensed and incorporated into everything from set-top boxes to mobile phones.

INPUT/OUTPUT

1 Centronics
2 RS432
3 RGB
4 Econet (Acorn network)
5 Four expansion slots (400 series)
6 Mouse
7 Headphone jack

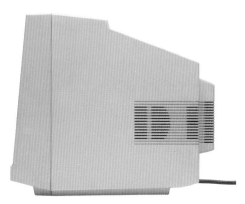

DID YOU KNOW?

The Archimedes range included models with grey function keys targeted at the wider market and the familiar red function keys of the BBC Micro for the education sector. Acorn continued with this colour coding on later single-box A3000 series computers, with green keys for an ill-fated model targeted at the home games market, red for education and grey for the powerful A5000 and RiscPC systems. The sheer processing power of the Archimedes's RISC chip was often illustrated via two famous software demonstrations. One was the speedy generation of fractal-based Mandelbrot sets, while the second was the excellent 3D Lander game, programmed by David Braben of Elite fame (*see p82*).

After leaving Apple in 1985, Steve Jobs cofounded NeXT computer with five key former Apple employees: Susan Barnes for finance, Bud Tribble for software, Rich Page and George Crow for hardware and Daniel Lewin for his experience as Apple's head of education. Education was Jobs's target, making Lewin's experience invaluable. Lewin had gotten Macs into use at twenty-four elite universities and started a programme where they could be sold to students at a significant discount. The idea was that top students of today would become business leaders of tomorrow, and they would remain faithful to the computers they'd gained experience with. Furious that Jobs had essentially poached its education department, Apple filed a lawsuit against NeXT, but dropped it four months later.

Jobs set about developing his vision of a no-expense-spared, high-end workstation. A fully automated, state-of-the-art production line was built, the NeXT offices were lavishly remodelled with top-of-the-range furniture, and Yale art professor Paul Rand was paid $100,000 to come up with a logo.

After spending $7 million of his own money in just over a year, Jobs looked for outside investment. H. Ross Perot, multimillionaire founder of EDS and future US presidential candidate, invested $20 million for a 16 percent stake. Canon later invested $100 million for a sixth of the company.

NeXT Cube

Manufacturer: NeXT
Model: Cube

Launched: October 1988
Country of Origin: USA

COMPANY HISTORY

During the spring and summer of 1985, tensions between Apple founder Steve Jobs and company boss John Sculley grew to a point that Jobs was asked to step down from running the Macintosh division. Feeling betrayed by both the company he founded and the man he later hired to run it, Jobs plotted to create an ultimate Macintosh that Apple itself could never realize: a high-end workstation aimed at the educational market.

Toward the end of July 1985, Jobs put the wheels in motion. He started by selling 782,000 of his Apple shares to raise $11.2 million, followed by a further 500,000 worth $7.4 million. This still left him as Apple's largest shareholder, with 8.9 percent of the company. Then, on 12th September he announced his resignation to the Apple board, explaining he'd start a new venture that would be complementary to Apple rather than competing with it. He'd also be taking a few Apple employees with him.

SPECIFICATION

CPU model: Motorola 68030
Speed: 25MHz
RAM: 8MB
Special features: All black system, CD-quality sound, rewritable magneto-optical disks, display PostScript (on later models)
Local price at launch: $6500

NeXT
Cube

Manufacturer: NeXT
Model: Cube

WHAT HAPPENED NEXT

Three years after Jobs quit Apple, NeXT finally unveiled its workstation. An all-black cube with matching monitor, keyboard and mouse, it looked stunning. The internals were impressive, and the NeXTStep operating system was superb.

NeXT had created the ultimate educational workstation, but sadly, at $6,500, few students could afford it. In March 1989, the Cube was made available to non-educational users for $9,995, but Sun already had the high-end market tied up. Even the follow-up NeXT Station with colour and display PostScript couldn't turn its fortunes.

NeXT's saviour was its OS, adapted to run on numerous platforms. Keen for its own multitasking OS for the Mac, Apple bought NeXT over its rival Be in 1996 for $400 million; the deal included Jobs as consultant. After later serving as interim CEO for two and a half years, Jobs retook Apple's reins in January 2000.

Following Steve Jobs's return to Apple, a PowerMac Cube was launched in July 2000. Sales were disappointing; the machine was regarded as an expensive luxury compared to the cheap, all-in-one iMac the market wanted.

INPUT/OUTPUT

1 3x free NeXTbus connectors
2 SCSI (Internal)
3 SCSI 2 (External)
4 DSP
5 Video out
6 Proprietary NeXT printer
7 2x RS232
8 Ethernet

DID YOU KNOW?

Steve Jobs is also CEO of computer-graphics movie company Pixar. Back in 1979, George Lucas recruited several experts in computer graphics to join his special-effects company Industrial Light & Magic (ILM). This department produced several pioneering sequences, including the Genesis demonstration in *Star Trek II: The Wrath of Khan*.

By the end of 1985, though, Lucas needed to raise money following his divorce, so he put the division up for sale for $30 million. Steve Jobs visited Lucasfilm and was mightily impressed, but the asking price was too high. After several buyers fell through, Jobs negotiated a sale for $10 million in February 1986.

His investment took a while to pay off, but in 1995, Pixar released *Toy Story* through Disney as the first fully computer-generated feature film. Directed by John Lasseter, it was the highest-grossing film that year, earning $362 million worldwide. Pixar's subsequent movies and IPO brought Jobs great wealth and the status of a Hollywood player.

post-history: 1989 to present day

As the 1980s drew to a close, the writing was on the wall for proprietary computers – at least as far as homes and businesses were concerned. While many systems of the Eighties carved successful niches as low-cost alternatives for domestic or educational markets, they had gained only a temporary stay of execution.

A combination of cheaper components and increased competition gradually drove the prices of PC clones down to a point where they simply became affordable and sensible options for both homes and schools, in addition to their original business customers.

By the early Nineties, almost every computer company was producing IBM compatibles, rendering proprietary systems from the Eighties extinct. Apple was the exception with its Macintosh range, which continues to this day – although it holds only a fraction of the market. While Mac owners passionately believe theirs is the superior platform, it's interesting to note Macs have long been compatible with files created on IBM clones.

Apple actually dabbled with Mac clones in the mid-Nineties, but withdrew licensing when its own hardware sales were threatened. A decade earlier, IBM also lost out thanks to clones of its PCs, but as they were legally reverse-engineered, the company couldn't prevent their rise. Indeed, by the late Eighties, some of the bigger clones had grown to a point where they were defining new standards. Others, like Dell, founded in 1984, pioneered the use of direct mail-order sales to keep costs down.

Many believe the domination of a single platform has stifled innovation, and that the IBM PC was far from the best technology to standardize on. While the latter assertion is debatable, the fact remains that the earlier period of incompatible systems was simply unsustainable. A standard needed to be adopted in order for the industry to enjoy greater competition, and circumstances made the IBM PC the best overall

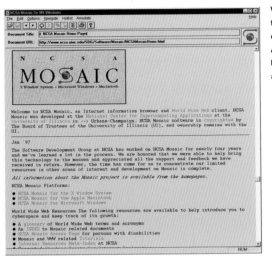

Version 1.0 of NCSA Mosaic, the first Web browser to combine text and graphics. Arguably this was the beginning of the Internet as we know it today.

choice. Far from killing off the inventive spirit, standardizing on the PC allowed software developers to concentrate on a single platform rather than spreading themselves thin.

While the first homes to buy PCs had little choice but to run traditional office applications, a new development in the mid-Nineties would drive computers into over half the households of developed countries.

Back in 1980, Tim Berners-Lee took a job at CERN, in Switzerland, as a contract programmer. He worked on ways to store information with random links and had a breakthrough in 1989 while at the European Particle Physics Laboratory.

Berners-Lee proposed a means by which any information accessible on a network could be known by a unique identifier. These identities could be used as addresses to locate specific pages of information wherever they might be. Better still, links to other addresses could allow an easy jump from one page to another, whether it was stored on the same computer or in machines on opposite sides of the planet. Berners-Lee had essentially invented the World Wide Web and the means by which it could be navigated.

In 1990, he wrote a program that ran on Steve Jobs's NeXT workstation, offering a point-and-click editor for these "hypertext" links. The following year, he released it as an open system for the high-energy physics and NeXT communities, and as demand for accessing "web" servers increased, he formed the World Wide Web Consortium (W3C) to define its future development.

To access the Web, you needed a physical connection to the Internet – but in the early Nineties, this meant renting a leased line at a cost of up to $30,000 USD per year. Homes and small businesses could not afford these connections, but they could use modems and residential telephones to dial into dedicated Bulletin Board Systems, or BBSs. The only problem was that many BBSs were housed in other countries,

thereby demanding expensive international calls. In contrast, the Internet only required a local connection, after which you could connect freely to machines anywhere in the world. The problem with the Internet, however, remained the high cost of a leased line to make that initial connection.

Regular visitors to BBSs discussed ways around the problem. The general consensus was that, barring the cost of the leased line, it would be possible for multiple people to enjoy Internet access if they all dialled into a computer connected to the line.

Then in 1992, Cliff Stanford, a regular of the UK online conference CiX, suggested the cost of a leased line could be covered if just 200 people offered to pay £10 per month for shared dialup access. His proposal, entitled "tenner_a_month," had enough subscribers for Demon Internet to be launched on 1st June 1992. This model for subscription-based dialup access to a shared leased line became the foundation of Internet service providers to this day.

The general public now had affordable access to the Internet, but how would they navigate it? Arguably, the first Web-browsing application was Mosaic, developed in 1993 by a group of students at the University of Illinois. The team behind Mosaic was led by Marc Andreessen, who in 1994 joined Silicon Graphics founder Jim Clarke to form Netscape.

Netscape Navigator was the leading Web browser for many years, until Microsoft launched Navigator's rival, Internet Explorer, in 1996. By the end of its first year, IE was on version three, and Netscape had serious competition. Crucially, future versions of Microsoft Windows came with Internet Explorer installed free, encouraging many people to adopt it rather than pay for, or even download, free alternatives. While allowing Microsoft to quickly dominate the Web-browsing market, this strategy later landed the company in court for anticompetitive behaviour.

post-history: 1989 to present day

Whichever software was being used, though, people's hunger to access the Internet to browse the Web, send email and buy goods online drove PC sales through the roof. Indeed, many online sales were actually to buy more PCs: Dell launched its site in 1994 and was selling online two years later. That said, PCs weren't strictly necessary for accessing the Web, but they provided one of the easiest and most effective online experiences.

While Microsoft put Internet Explorer in every copy of Windows, Apple, too, exploited the exploding popularity of the Internet by branding its new all-in-one range, launched in 1998, as the iMac. While the pastel-coloured translucent iMac cases designed by Jonathan Ives were responsible for many sales, Apple's new all-in-one also drove the industry adoption of several new technologies, while dumping old ones like the floppy drive.

The Universal Serial Bus, or USB, was first popularly implemented in the iMac, offering just one type of plug to connect all manner of devices, from keyboards to cameras and printers. Better still, not only was USB faster than the wealth of ports it replaced, it allowed you to connect or disconnect devices without first switching the computer off. USB is now the universal standard for device connectivity on both Macs and PCs.

While accessing the Internet continues to drive many computer sales, the next phase is likely to be convergence with traditional consumer appliances. The concept of fridges and stereo systems enjoying PC-style connectivity and Internet access has long been touted, but it is only now beginning to be a realistic or compelling proposition thanks to several key technologies.

First is the advent of broadband, which has brought fast, unmetred Internet access into our homes. More importantly, it's allowed Internet access to be treated

Computer styling is becoming important across the market. Apple have led the field in innovative design, moving away from dull plastic cases in 1998 with the candy-coloured iMac and subsequently introducing the sleek metallic G5.

A vision of the future – the Internet fridge

like any other utility, on par with water, electricity or gas. A single pipe may enter our homes, but it's then redirected and shared throughout multiple rooms. Now, limiting Internet access to a single PC in the back room is essentially no different to only having just one sink or electrical point in your entire home. It would be insane not to distribute this resource.

Today, more than just PCs can go online. An increasing number of consumer appliances can also exploit the Internet – whether it's a console that lets you play head-to-head games with someone on the other side of the planet, set-top boxes downloading updated TV schedules, stereos streaming foreign radio stations or security cameras allowing you to keep an eye on your home while you're on holiday. And yes, there are even fridges that can monitor their contents, alert you to items going off and place orders for replacements.

Networking every appliance in your home is all very well, but no one wants miles of extra cabling. The second key technology, wireless networking, overcomes this problem. As its name suggests, wireless networking allows devices to be linked without cables. While starting as a technology to link laptops to corporate networks, wireless networking capabilities are increasingly found in a number of devices, including consumer appliances.

The third and most crucial technology of all, though, is one that will allow all these devices to communicate seamlessly without technical intervention. While far from complete at the time of writing, this final piece in the puzzle will marry the ease of consumer goods with the almost-limitless power of personal computers.

Over the past thirty years, personal computers have gone from kit-based, bare circuit boards to affordable machines that can edit home videos, process digital photos, store vast music collections and allow us to communicate quickly and easily with people all over the world. Many laughed at the original concept of PCs on every desk, yet over half the population of developed countries own them – and they say the best is yet to come. Here's to the next thirty years.

POSTSCRIPT

There might be a PC or Mac on your desk, but there's no need for home computers of the Eighties to become distant memories. Many live on today as emulators, which allow you to relive the fun using your current computer. Searching for emulators on the Web will direct you to lovingly programmed tributes to key computers and consoles of the Eighties.

Several museums are also now dedicated to old computer collections, two of which greatly helped me source products for this book (see acknowledgements for contact details). Private collectors can find many old machines for sale using online auctions like eBay. The PC may have long won the war, but it's ironic how much fun can be had pretending you're back in 1982.

index

190_191

acknowledgements

192

Thanks to the following innovators, who kindly consented to be interviewed for this book:

Sophie Wilson, Nick Toop, Steve Furber, Chris Turner, Roland Perry, Barry Muncaster, Paul Johnson, Everett Kasar, Kent Henscheid, John Law, Steve Vickers, Richard Altwasser, Paul Downham, David Rolfe, Dan Bricklin, David Karlin, Leonard Tramiel, Chuck Peddle, Rick Dickinson, Michael Tomczyk, Hermann Hauser, Lee Felsenstein, Sir Clive Sinclair, Hank Mishkoff, Steve Mayer, Noah Falstein, Steve O'Hara-Smith, John Grant, Duncan Smeed, Joe Decuir, Lyndon Davies, Jef Raskin, Albert Charpentier, Shiraz Shivji, Jim Westwood, Jack Tramiel and Julian Rangely.

Thanks also to the enthusiasts, historians and journalists for their memories and for documenting their tireless research:

Old Computers Museum: www.old-computers.com

Binary Dinosaurs: www.binary dinosaurs.co.uk

Planet Sinclair: www.nvg.ntnu.no/sinclair/contents.htm

Atari Museum: www.atarimuseum.com

IBM Archives: www-1.ibm.com/ibm/history

Intel Museum: www.intel.com/intel/intelis/museum

Blue Sky Rangers for IntelliVision: www.intellivisionlives.com

Microcomputer Timeline by Ken Polsson: www.islandnet.com/~kpolsson/comphist

Mick for Nascom: www.mixtel.pwp.blueyonder.co.uk

Bryan Roppolo for Texas Instruments: www.whtech.com/toucan

Gerald McMullon, ex-GBS and ex-editor of the Newbrain User Group

Tony Adams, *Einstein* magazine and Einstein User Group

Ken Ross for additional Tatung details

Michael S. Malone for "Infinite Loop"

Alan Deutschman for "The Second Coming of Steve Jobs"

Personal Computer World magazine

Masaaki Takeda at Sharp and the Sharp Museum

Additional thanks to Simon Rockman, Ian Betteridge, Rupert Goodwins, Jez San, Stan Veit, Roger Gann, John Shadbolt for the loan of his HP-85, Greg and Sam Elkin for the loan of their Tangerine Microtan 65, Pete French for the loan of his NeXT Cube, Keith Martin for the loan of his Apple Macintosh Plus, Richard Goodwin for the loan of his Acorn Archimedes, Aaron Timbrell of VirtualAcorn (www.virtualacorn.co.uk) for his RISC OS emulator, Holly Cudbill, *Personal Computer World* magazine for childhood inspiration, continued research and my very first job, Adam Juniper, Steve Luck and Alastair Campbell at ILEX for sharing my passion of retro computing and the presentation in this book, designer Jonathan Raimes and photographer Rob Turner.

Finally, major thanks for allowing us to photograph their collections are due to Simon Webb and the Swindon-based Museum of Computing (www.museum-of-computing.org.uk) and to John Sinclair and the Computer Museum at Bletchley (www.bletchleypark.org.uk).

Not forgetting everyone who worked on developing a home computer or video game console, in particular the teams at Atari, Apple, Commodore and Sinclair, and Ultimate Play the Game, whose *Jet-Pac*, *Atic-Atac*, and *Sabre Wulf Trilogy* were quite literally the most amazing games I have ever played.